D0923444

KATHRYN KUHLMAN:

The Woman Who Believes in Miracles

Also by the author

THE UNEXPLAINED

KATHRYN KUHLMAN:
The Woman Who Believes
in Miracles

by Allen Spraggett

The World Publishing Company
New York and Cleveland

Published by The World Publishing Company
2231 West 110th Street, Cleveland, Ohio 44102
Published simultaneously in Canada by
Nelson, Foster & Scott Ltd.

First printing—1970

Library of Congress Catalog Card Number: 71–103843
Printed in the United States of America

WORLD PUBLISHING
TIMES MIRROR

The author and publisher gratefully acknowledge
permission to reprint a selection from Gross,
The Case for Spiritual Healing, by permission of
Thomas Nelson and Sons.

for
STEPHEN, ALANNA, SANDRA, DENNIS,
AND KATHRYN

—my best achievements

Acknowledgments

My heartfelt thanks go to all those who spoke with me so willingly and gave permission for the use of their experiences in this book. I express special appreciation to the members of the medical fraternity quoted herein.

To Kathryn Kuhlman, of course, and to the members of her staff, I owe an incalculable debt. Marguerite Hartner, Miss Kuhlman's girl Friday, stands out. Needless to say, Kathryn Kuhlman bears no responsibility for any interpretations offered in this book.

Last but large is my gratitude to my editor, Katharine Kidde, without whose patient prodding and ever astute advice this book surely would never have seen the light of print.

Note to the Reader

Virtually all the cases reported in this book, even those mentioned more or less in passing, are based on interviews conducted by the author. In most instances they were tape recorded. A few of the interviews took place in April 1964, but most were in September and October 1968. The locales of the interviews were Pittsburgh and vicinity, Youngstown and Canton, Ohio, and Los Angeles and San Francisco.

Contents

Introduction

In 1947, after I returned to Pittsburgh from my tour of duty in the armed services, I began hearing stories about this woman Kathryn Kuhlman. Since I was traveling in medical circles, these stories, initially at least, were not very complimentary.

As the years went by, the stories persisted and grew. I even had patients who had been to Kathryn's services. Since they were seeing me they were those, naturally, who had not been healed, but despite this fact they all seemed to have been inspired by this woman and were devoted to her in an unusual way. I say unusual because there was nothing fanatical about their devotion and, oddly enough, they showed very little in the way of hard feelings that their wishes for peace of mind had not been granted. Instead, they all showed a determination to try harder to understand themselves and improve their attitudes in the hope that they eventually might obtain relief.

Miss Kuhlman's acceptance by the city and many of its people gradually reached unqualified proportions. This obviously was due to the fact that she was unquestionably helping people and doing it in such a way that many were deeply impressed by her sincerity and few, if any, seriously offended by her methods.

Her services are conducted with dignity, genuine warmth and, of all things, a real sense of humor. There is no attempt at self-glorification and she has a true understanding of the human nature of people's problems. This understanding I can only compare to that of Jesus: she, too, has the knack of giving simple answers to complicated questions.

The documentation of the fact that miracles do occur in Kathryn Kuhlman's ministry is a necessary first step toward understanding precisely what takes place in such occurrences. Documentation is necessary so that men of science can begin objectively to examine this phenomenon of miraculous healing in the hope that it can be more clearly understood and more widely used to help others.

I was impressed by the fact that some physicians must already understand this because one of the people at the healing service I attended had been brought by her physician, a medical doctor, who was willing to admit that in this case "medicine could help no more." Happily, this patient did receive her cure.

I am particularly pleased to have Mr. Spraggett raise the question of ESP phenomena and their relationship to the miraculous cures of Kathryn Kuhlman. Certainly the mind and its vast inner reaches are involved and the study of these healings should contribute significantly to our understanding of ESP.

But this is going to take more than only "men of science" because, you see, whenever one gets into the study of ESP, unless he is content to spend his whole life counting card guesses, dice throws, etc., sooner or later he must bump heads with the concept of the existence of the soul, the survival of the personality after death, and many other basic religious tenets.

I have been a student and observer in this field for some time and my conclusion at this point is that the purpose of ESP talent is to enable an individual to make closer contact with his own soul and if this is not achieved in a sincere way the talent usually begins to fade or at least becomes quite erratic. Because of this I feel that the current movement towards joint work by the fields of psychiatry, psychology, and religion should be intensified. There is a great deal to be learned from the union of these disciplines in terms of real ways for developing individual personalities and helping them grow. Man does have a soul, you see, and this soul *is* the basis of his personality, and the sooner we understand this the better we are going to be at helping the sick in body as well as in mind.

Miss Kuhlman herself indicates that although she is at times overwhelmed by the physical healings which take place, she is much more awed when a soul has been touched and a life changed. Perhaps quoting one of the witnesses in a Kathryn Kuhlman service would get this point across best. This woman, who, as far as she is concerned, was plucked from the door of death by an unusually dramatic healing several months before, testified: "I'm ashamed to have had to find God in this fashion."

In Mr. Spraggett's book, the product of considerable investigation, we have an unbiased picture of Kathryn Kuhlman's work and its results, both good and bad, without exaggeration. This book certainly demonstrates that at least some of the miracles are phenomena which cannot be explained in the light of current medical knowledge. The fact that others of them can be explained by a dramatic change of heart and mind seems to be well understood by all concerned, including Miss Kuhlman and her staff. They seem to understand as well that a few of the healings are histrionics on the part of the "cured" individual. This understanding in no way detracts from the fact that some of Kathryn Kuhlman's miracles are really just that— miracles.

W. LINDSAY JACOB, M.D.
Pittsburgh, Pa.

Editor's Note: Dr. Jacob is a psychiatrist in private practice in Pittsburgh and a frequent lecturer in clinical psychiatry.

1

A Miracle Service

The time: Sunday. Noon.

The place: Los Angeles. Outside the Shrine Auditorium.

The event: The regular monthly "miracle service" of Pittsburgh's Kathryn Kuhlman.

An enormous crowd has gathered, and it's still two hours before the miracles are supposed to start.

Here, in the cult capital of the world, mecca of every crazy sect and self-proclaimed messiah, this city which has seen everything that calls itself religion and seen through most of it, crowds still turn out to see miracles.

It is a mixed crowd. Long-haired hippies, looking like parodies of themselves in garish costumes and bare feet, rub shoulders with dignified dowagers. The little old ladies are here, the kind who live in one room and cook their meals on hotplates. And there are young couples with children, gray-suited businessmen, students, clergymen in dog collars, and even one or two faded movie stars hiding behind dark glasses.

The old-time religion is said to attract its followers mainly from the lower socioeconomic groups, but this

1

crowd doesn't look undernourished. On the whole, it's the kind you might find outside a movie theater on a Saturday night.

Some of these people, says a friendly policeman mopping his brow, have been waiting since nine o'clock. Why, last week the Bolshoi Ballet was here from Moscow but they didn't draw crowds like this. He strolls off, shaking his head.

But the Bolshoi Ballet doesn't offer miracles, and in Kathryn Kuhlman's meetings cripples are supposed to get up and walk and the blind receive their sight. The crowds are here to see these things for themselves. And some, sick and deformed, are hoping they may be among the miracles.

By one o'clock the crowd has swollen to such proportions—fifteen thousand the policeman estimates, and there are only half that many seats inside—that the doors are opened a half hour early. A human tidal wave rushes into the mammoth auditorium, drowning it. Ten minutes later the doors are shut, with seven thousand still outside clamoring to get in.

"We've been known to separate husbands and wives," quips one of the ushers as he wrestles a door shut.

The sick are very much in evidence. By the looks of them, there will have to be some spectacular miracles. Some are in wheel chairs, others carry heavy steel braces on their legs, crouch over canes, hobble on crutches. There are a few stretcher cases, one with tubes up his nose and in his arm, as if he has come straight from the hospital. The blind, the deaf-mute, the spastic, the congenitally deformed—they are all here, seeking a miracle.

Was it this way in Galilee two thousand years ago?

The service is scheduled to begin in an hour, but Kathryn Kuhlman's motto is: "When the house is full, we start!"

A gray-haired man in a dark suit walks on stage with a springy tread. This is Dr. Arthur Metcalfe, English-born former conductor of the Pittsburgh Civic Chorus and for fourteen years Kathryn Kuhlman's director of music. At his signal, the three hundred members of the choir rise in their places. His hands poised for the downbeat, he waits for a moment, like a diver about to plunge. Then the choir erupts into song. The music wells up and rushes at the congregation like an explosion. Upward-spiralling, the music reaches an ecstatic crescendo.

Does any church choir sing like this?

Abruptly the mood of the music changes and now the hymn is quiet, gentle, but with undertones of deep feeling moving beneath the placid surface. It is a familiar hymn and there are nods and smiles from the congregation.

"That's her song, Miss Kuhlman's," an elderly lady in the front row whispers to her neighbor. "Here she comes."

The evangelist appears from the wings with dramatic suddenness, as though she had materialized out of thin air. She wears a dress of dazzling white silk trimmed with gold. For a long moment she stands unmoving at the corner of the stage, as if frozen in time and space, a tall figure, slim as an arrow, with long auburn hair that glints under the lights. Then she walks briskly to the microphone in the center of the stage, taking long strides. Her smile is blinding. Charisma pours from her in almost visible rays. So powerful is her magnetism that the congregation leaps to its feet as one person and bursts into tremendous applause, a tumult of adulation.

The ovation ceases abruptly as Kathryn Kuhlman leads the choir in the singing of her theme hymn, the words clear and deliberate:

> He touched me, oh, He touched me,
> And, oh, the joy that filled my soul!
> Something happened and now I know
> He touched me, and made me whole . . .

The huge congregation sings it, once, twice, over and over. It becomes a chant, an incantation, hypnotic in its effect. The emotional temperature rises. Tears lie close to the surface. I think: This is like Lourdes, like the chanting of the "Ave Maria," the same rhythmic repetition, the same almost unbearably intense feeling.

The evangelist, no longer singing, stands in a cruciform posture, her arms flung wide, her face upturned, lips moving as though in prayer. Her face—it must be an optical illusion—actually appears to give off light. She seems oblivious of her surroundings, caught up in a transport, lost in her personal love affair with God.

Then, in the tone of an oracle, she spoke.

"There is power in the name of Jesus," intoned the husky, vibrant voice. "Yes,. there is power in the name of Jesus."

A hush settled over the vast congregation, punctuated only by random coughing and murmurings of "Dear Jesus."

Then Kathryn Kuhlman prayed aloud: "We know, Father, yes, we know that miracles are going to happen in this place today. Oh, we feel the blessed presence of Thy Holy Spirit. We promise to give you all the praise, all the glory, for what is about to happen here. Pour out your power on us, for Jesus' sake."

In an abrupt change of mood the evangelist was now folksy, welcoming the congregation to the service, especially those from distant places. Where do you come from? In response there were shouts of "England," "Japan," "Brazil," and a dozen other countries.

"We've got the whole United Nations here!" exulted Kathryn Kuhlman and the crowd enjoyed a chuckle with her.

With yet another change of pace, the evangelist now was telling about a miraculous healing that happened in this auditorium a month ago. A woman from Oklahoma came to the service hobbling on crutches and went away carrying them.

"And she's here today," the evangelist said, "to show that people who get healed in these services stay healed. Here she comes now!"

A matronly woman in a dark blue dress, her face beaming, fairly bounced onto the stage holding aloft a pair of crutches. As Kathryn Kuhlman greeted her with outstretched arms, the organ boomed a mighty chord and the congregation gave her an ovation.

"Tell us what happened to you," said the evangelist.

The woman spoke into the microphone, her voice tremulous but clear.

"When I came to the service here last month, I couldn't walk without these crutches. The reason was that I didn't have enough bones in my feet to support my weight. In fact, all I have left are the bones in my heel and my big toe. Yet, since my healing, I can even wiggle my toes."

The evangelist laughed and asked for a demonstration. Slipping off a shoe, the woman vigorously wiggled her toes.

"She's doing it," the evangelist exclaimed, "she's doing it!"

The congregation burst into another ovation.

"The trouble, you see, was that I had tumors in both feet," the woman continued. "I had surgery twelve times on one foot and fifteen times on the other. They removed the metatarsal heads, the balls of my feet, and other bones too. The soles were then rebuilt with skin taken from my stomach."

"And how did this affect you?" the evangelist asked.

"Well, as I said, I couldn't walk without crutches. The pain in my left foot especially was so bad that I couldn't bear the slightest weight on it. Now I can do this."

The woman stamped her left foot on the floor—hard. The congregation applauded again and Kathryn Kuhlman beamed. Then she spoke to a distinguished-looking man behind her on the stage.

"Dr. Biery," she motioned to him to come forward, "you examined this lady last month during the service. I want you to tell us as a medical man what you think about this."

Turning to the congregation, she said: "This is Dr. Martin Biery, a surgeon who operated on more than seven hundred spines while on the staff of the Veterans' Hospital in Long Beach. Take the microphone, Dr. Biery, and tell us about this case."

"When I examined the lady a month ago I found that— just as she said—virtually all the bones in her feet were missing," Dr. Biery said, in a quiet, matter-of-fact voice.

"Now, when you destroy a major portion of the weight-bearing part of the foot you make normal walking impossible. There is great pain and tenderness, for one thing. But when I examined this lady during last month's service there was no pain or tenderness in her feet at all."

Kathryn Kuhlman turned to the woman: "Show us again how you can walk."

The lady strode across the stage and back with the heavy tread of a drill sergeant.

"What do you say to that, Dr. Biery?" demanded the evangelist.

He shook his head, and murmured barely audibly: "In all honesty I can only say that has to come from God."

"Yes, that *has* to come from God," intoned Kathryn Kuhlman, taking it up like a litany. "That *has* to come from God."

She lifted her eyes and stretched her arms upward: "Dear Jesus, all we can say is thank you, thank you, thank you . . . for another miracle."

At this point tears came readily. The evangelist was visibly weeping, the woman who had been healed was sobbing loudly into a handkerchief, and Dr. Biery covered his eyes with his hand. Many in the congregation were crying too.

A moment later the tears turned to chuckles. In another sudden change of pace Kathryn Kuhlman was giving a colorful description of an incident that had happened a short time before in Pittsburgh, where she holds regular weekly healing meetings.

"Unknown to me a Roman Catholic priest from New York was in our miracle service," the evangelist said. "Something happened to him during that service—something wonderful. This is how he expressed it in a letter to me: 'Dear Miss Kuhlman, All praise to the eternal Father. All praise to Jesus Christ. All praise to the Holy Spirit. The Spirit has come to me!'

"A short time later he wrote again, inviting me to hold services in his town. He said, 'I'm sorry that it isn't possible for me to invite you to preach in my church. But if you come, I'll rent the auditorium, I'll back you to the hilt, so that others might experience what I've experienced.' "

The evangelist added, with a chuckle: "This reminds

me of the little Catholic girl who came to a miracle service with her mother and said, 'Oh mommy, wouldn't Mrs. Kuhlman make a wonderful Father!' "

The laughter subsided quickly as the evangelist, like quicksilver, again slid into a different mood. She grew very serious, her voice low, intimate, urgent.

"My friends"—one had to strain to hear her—"I am sensitive enough to the Holy Spirit to know that wonderful things are going to happen today. Miracles—very special ones—are going to happen in this place this afternoon.

"The light of God's love is in this place. But it's dark outside and it's getting darker. There's so much hate out there, so much greed out there, so much misunderstanding out there. And the only hope we have is the love of God.

"That's why you're here today, to see the love and power of God at work. You wouldn't walk across the street just to see me, Kathryn Kuhlman. I know that . . ."

The evangelist's voice, almost a whisper, trailed away. She seemed to be struggling to control herself.

"What can I do? I can't preach. I can't sing. I can't do anything special. I have no talent. I can just love you."

Tears were running down her cheeks and most of the congregation appeared to be in tears. An usher, a faultlessly dressed man in his forties, dabbed his eyes with a silk handkerchief. A little old Negro lady sat rocking in her seat with her hands cupped over her face and tears trickling out between her fingers. Choir members, men and women, cried openly. This was more emotion than one finds in the usual church service. But there was no hysteria.

The evangelist murmured: "I love God with every atom of my being. And I know that in this place today the Holy Spirit is moving. . . . Gently, gently. . . . Get your mind off Kathryn Kuhlman, my friend. Don't think about your faith. *Don't think*. Just get your eyes on God. Think of God. Get lost in God. . . ."

At this point, the emotion in the evangelist's voice was electric. The service was approaching its climax. The atmosphere was tense with expectation. Old-timers were waiting for what they knew was going to happen any moment now.

Then it happened. "The Power" struck.

"I rebuke those migraine headaches," exclaimed Kathryn Kuhlman. She was leaning over the lectern, gripping it as though for support, her eyes shut. She pointed to the first gallery.

In just that instant somebody in the balcony here was healed of migraine. It came instantaneously.

"A second person is being healed—another migraine. I rebuke that allergy that causes those migraine headaches. I rebuke it!"

The evangelist's voice rose to a shout.

"Somebody's ear has opened. It happened not more than two minutes ago. On the ground floor, over to my right. A middle-aged woman. You didn't even expect to be healed but you are."

The words now were tumbling from the evangelist almost too fast to follow. It was like automatic speaking, as though her tongue were racing ahead of her mind. She called out healings of spinal disease, of blindness, of cancer of the lungs, of a crippled leg.

The ushers were prowling the aisles like hunting dogs on the lookout for prey. They were searching for the cases of healing announced by the evangelist. Where was the person healed of migraine? The woman healed of deafness?

(Kathryn Kuhlman says that she herself cannot explain

how she knows "the exact body being healed and the very disease in that body," but she insists that she does know. "The Holy Spirit tells me," is all she can offer.)

She was racing on, caught up now in a mystic thrall, apparently oblivious of everyone and everything around her.

"Diabetes is being healed. To my right in the first balcony somebody is being healed of diabetes at this very moment. Don't be frightened, that heat in your body is the power of God.

"And a growth has disappeared. It's a man up there in the top balcony. Examine your leg and you'll find that the growth that was behind your knee is gone. God has healed you while you sat there.

"Somebody down here on the ground floor just got her sense of smell back after years. It came as suddenly as that, while I was speaking.

"And an extreme case of sinus is instantly gone. You had some kind of operation on your nose in the last two months but it didn't help. Now that sinus is completely healed.

"A blind eye is clearing. Somebody has a cataract and that cataract is slipping. It's the right eye. That's up in the first balcony to my left. The cataract is melting even as I speak. . . ."

The evangelist staggered as if she might fall, clutching at the lectern to steady herself.

"Oh, there's so much Power here today!" she exclaimed. "It's everywhere! The Power's everywhere!"

Now the procession of the healed, wanting to testify to what had happened to them, started. Even as they began to file onto the stage, escorted by ushers, the evangelist called out other healings—asthma ("It's a woman, in the first balcony halfway back"), heart disease ("A man who's

been an invalid for years; you know you've been healed
because suddenly you can take big breaths without pain"),
a spinal disorder ("On the ground floor, a man; you know
something's happened because a moment ago you felt this
terrific heat in your back"), cancer ("A woman with a
tumor of the breast; it's gone, feel it and find out").

The first usher introduced his healing cases to the evangelist: "These two ladies were healed of migraine headaches, Miss Kuhlman. Their headaches left as you called out
the healings."

Kathryn Kuhlman laid her hands on the heads of the
two women—and they instantly collapsed.

This dramatic phenomenon—which the true believers
call "going down under The Power"—is a curious but
constant feature of the Kuhlman meetings. Suggestion?
Hysteria? Or, as the believers insist, a supernatural manifestation? At any rate, so common is the phenomenon that
there is an official catcher whose duty it is to prevent those
who fall from injuring themselves. He hovers behind everybody for whom Kathryn Kuhlman prays, waiting for them
to collapse, as they usually do.

Some fall with their backs rigid, as in a cataleptic swoon
or hypnotic trance. Others double over, as though they had
been punched in the solar plexus. Still others crumple like
empty sacks.

The sensations experienced by the subjects are variously
described as "like being hit by lightning," "a thousand
needles going through you all at once," "a cool breeze
blows over you and then you're out," "an immense peace-
fulness." Most of those who experience the phenomenon
seem to agree that it leaves a feeling of well-being and
euphoria that sometimes lasts for several days.

One woman testified to having recovered her sense of

smell after twenty years, and added that she came from
Kathryn Kuhlman's home state of Missouri, to which the
evangelist retorted: "Well, if someone from Missouri can
be healed, God can heal anyone!"

A little girl was brought forward by her mother who
described her as having been "almost blind" from a blood
clot on the optic nerve. Now, she said, the child could see
perfectly.

Kathryn Kuhlman summoned a woman from the back
of the stage and introduced her as Dr. Viola Frymann, a
physician and surgeon from La Jolla, California. Miss
Kuhlman invited her to examine the child.

Holding up ten fingers, Dr. Frymann asked the little
girl to count them. The girl counted to ten. The doctor
moved a little further away and held up two fingers and
the child counted to two. This continued for several minutes, the doctor gradually increasing the distance and vary-
ing the number of fingers. Then she talked with the child's
mother.

"This child's vision is now apparently normal," Dr.
Frymann reported to the congregation. "Under ordinary
circumstances a blood clot on the optic nerve does not
clear of its own accord."

A man in his forties testified that he had been healed of
a spinal disorder.

"A back infection had eaten out one of my vertebrae,"
he told the congregation, "and I had a disc removed three
months ago. I was in agonizing pain during the service but
felt instant relief the same moment I heard Miss Kuhlman
say, 'A man with a spinal condition is being healed.' "

To demonstrate his cure, the man, at the evangelist's
request, bent and touched his toes several times.

Kathryn Kuhlman asked Dr. Biery his medical opinion.

"Well," he responded, "I can only say that what this

man has just done is medically impossible. I know a great deal about spinal disorders and when a disc has been recently removed, any motion causes exquisite pain."

A seven-year-old girl, brought to the platform by her parents, was said to have been healed of cerebral palsy. From birth, her parents told the congregation, the child's left arm had been paralyzed and her left leg twisted, with the foot turned in severely, causing her to walk with a pronounced limp. During the miracle service, said the parents, the girl's paralyzed arm suddenly became free so that she could move it at will. At the same moment, her leg straightened.

Dr. Frymann examined the child, questioning the parents as she did so. Then Kathryn Kuhlman scooped the little girl up in her arms, murmuring: "Jesus loves you, and we love you."

Dr. Frymann gave her opinion of the case: "This child, her parents tell me, has cerebral palsy. I can only call what appears to have happened to her in this service medically extraordinary, to say the least. And it is particularly impressive because a young child does not respond hysterically under powerful emotion as an adult might."

The procession of those testifying to healings continued. A boy with only 40 percent vision in one eye had experienced a great improvement, declared his mother. A child able to distinguish only light and darkness now was said to be able to see forms and colors. A college student shook his head wonderingly as he reported that his fingers, previously gnarled by arthritis, were supple. A minister averred that seven "floaters"—permanent black specks in the field of vision resulting from hemorrhage in the eye—had disappeared after fifteen years.

At one point in the service a young man, apparently in his early twenties, wearing a cast on one leg, rushed down the aisle shouting: "Kathryn, Kathryn, let me touch you! I need The Power! Kathryn!" Intercepted by the ushers, he was forcibly restrained from hurling himself at the evangelist's feet. Kathryn Kuhlman, busy praying for others on the stage, appeared not to notice the commotion and the excitable young man was led, weeping, back to his seat.

It was now almost five o'clock. This incredible religious exercise—surely unparalleled anywhere—had been going on for three and a half hours. The evangelist, who had been active for that entire period, looked as fresh and vital as when she started. And the service was not over. Kathryn Kuhlman had one important piece of spiritual business yet to attend to.

"Wonderful as physical healing is, it's secondary to the healing of the soul," she told the congregation. "I believe in salvation from sin as a definite experience—an experience through which you can pass from death unto life, and be no longer under the bondage of sin.

"You can be transformed in a moment by the Spirit of God and become a new creature in Christ . . ."

Her voice now was soft, tender, wooing.

"Come," she coaxed, "come and accept Christ."

And they came. Her words reached out and touched people's heartstrings, pulling them out of their seats.

Streaming down the aisles, they came. Almost running in their eagerness, they came. Dazed, as if only half aware of what they were doing, they came. Smiling, they came. Weeping, they came. Old people, they came. Young hippies, in jeans and with bare feet, they came.

Drawn, as if by a magnet, they stood at the feet of the madonnalike figure in white who transformed that enormous auditorium, used to ballets and circuses, into a shrine, a place to find God.

The evangelist prayed aloud that each one of these

penitents would receive the Holy Spirit. Then she moved among those on the platform, conferring The Power by laying her hands on them. As she did—down they went. The stage was littered with prostrate forms.

This was the most curious of a series of curious spectacles. An observer fighting to remain objective probably would interpret the whole service either as an orgy of unproductive emotionalism, a demonstration of deep and fervent religious faith, or an exercise in mass psychosomatics. The choice would depend presumably on the observer's prejudices and whether or not the results of the service—notably the physical healings—were enduring.

But whatever his personal predilections, an observer would be unlikely to dispute that a Kathryn Kuhlman miracle service was a unique religious phenomenon.

Now, almost four hours after opening the service, the evangelist was bringing it to a close. Her batteries were obviously depleted, but her voice was still vibrant: "Those of you who have been healed, go to your doctor and get medical documentation. And remember, Kathryn Kuhlman had nothing to do with your healing. Know that! It was all God's doing. Give Him the glory. God bless you!"

The congregation said "Amen," the organ boomed, the choir chanted a benediction, and the figure in white vanished from the stage.

Another miracle service was over.

2

A Reporter Among the Faith Healers

How does a newspaperman get interested in faith healing, enough to write a book about it? That question may have occurred to you about this book and me.

Well, the fact that I have a background in the ministry may make the matter somewhat more explicable. But before you assume that I'm going to invoke a categorical imperative bearing on a great mission, let me confess that I enjoy my research into such anomalies as ESP and miraculous healings. It is for me what stamp collecting, learning Esperanto, or breeding mutations among red-eyed fruit flies in the basement is for some other people. Miracles are more exciting than fruit flies.

But there's more to it than that. As a thinking person I wonder about the meaning of life. And in faith healing I find a clue to that meaning—just as, if you like, the perturbation of Mercury was a clue that all was not well with the Newtonian view of the universe. Let me explain.

When Einstein came up with his fairly weird (by the scientific standards of that day) General Theory of Relativity, one thing in its favor was that it solved a puzzle which had long confounded astronomers—the eccentric behavior of Mercury. This planet had a peculiar irregularity in its orbit—slight but exasperating—which classic mechanics couldn't explain but which Einstein's new laws of gravitation explained very nicely indeed.

Miraculous healing is another Mercury. It doesn't fit into the framework of today's science. If such things as miracles happen, the universe and man must be different from what contemporary scientific doctrine says.

Years ago, then, I set out to try to answer the question: Do miracles happen? That quest led me to revival tents, shrines, medical consulting rooms, and hypnotists' parlors. Eventually it led to the woman this book is mainly about, the greatest spiritual healer of our time—Kathryn Kuhlman.

Here you will read about some of her inexplicable healings, documented with names, dates, places, and medical attestations.

But let me begin nearer the beginning. . . .

About twenty years ago, faith healing received some unwelcome publicity when a teen-aged diabetic in a small Ontario town died after giving up her insulin, allegedly at the exhortation of a tent-meeting revivalist. In the resulting hue and cry there was a proposal to prosecute the faith healer, but the legal consensus was that ultimate responsibility for the death rested on the girl herself and her parents.

However, the incident did underscore one of the hazards of religious healing ministries: that people may be misled into neglecting medical treatment, sometimes with disastrous consequences.

My personal experiences with faith healers, including those I've observed as an investigative reporter, have been considerable and, in many cases, negative.

Well do I remember my disillusionment when, as a teen-
ager, I attended a healing service in Toronto conducted by
a revivalist named A. C. Valdez. The climax of the meeting came when a young boy, at the healer's behest, threw
down his crutches and strode briskly across the platform.
The crowd went wild. Some jumped up and down, waving
handkerchiefs and shouting: "It's a miracle!" Others, awed
by the wonder of it, gave themselves over to ecstasy and
mumbled in unknown tongues.

My reaction, although I was open-minded about miracles, was considerably more critical. The boy, to be sure,
had walked without his crutches, but it seemed to me that
he had a limp. I wanted to be sure.

After the meeting was dismissed, I waited near the platform and presently saw the boy emerge from behind the
stage accompanied by his father. He was back on his
crutches.

"He wasn't healed, then?" I asked.

"Nope," said the father, shaking his head sadly. "Just
all stirred up."

That was the death of my first healing miracle. And, as
it turned out, only one of a number of such experiences.

In August 1963, Rev. Oral Roberts of Tulsa, Oklahoma,
the high priest of contemporary big-shot faith healers, descended on Toronto like a ball of fire. Ten thousand persons every night packed his "canvas cathedral," as Roberts
called the huge tent in which he held his meetings. Night
after night I watched as the lame, the blind, and the deaf
filed past him in the ritual of prayer and the laying on of
hands.

Were any really healed?

"Not everybody I pray for is healed," Roberts told me
when I put the question to him. "I don't know how many

are healed. You might as well ask a doctor how many of the people he treats are cured.

"I do know that in myself I couldn't heal a fly, but to God"—he piously rolled his eyes upwards—"no disease is incurable."

Bluntly I told Oral Roberts that there were features of his ministry which raised grave questions in my mind. One was his frequent reference to "demons," and his horrific practice of "casting out demons" from hysterical persons, while adjuring members of the congregation to keep their heads down lest the departing devil enter into them.

The practice of requiring people to sign cards describing their ailments before admitting them to the healing line to be prayed for also bothered me. It could be a ploy to screen the easy cases from the difficult ones, making sure that the evangelist was not confronted by persons who were unlikely to respond to his particular brand of shock therapy.

I took particular exception to the custom of segregating the seriously ill in an "invalids' tent," away from the prying eyes of the public. The evangelist paid a hasty visit to this tent after the main service, moving rapidly among the pathetic cases—wheel-chair cripples, the horribly deformed, the chronically bedridden—laying his hands on each one and saying a perfunctory prayer.

Oral Roberts' associates, I discovered, did not take kindly to a newspaperman poking around the invalids' tent, but my persistence gained me admittance over their objections. Not one of the invalids I observed showed the slightest improvement after the evangelist's brief visit.

When I mentioned to Oral Roberts that my fairly close scrutiny of his ministry in Toronto had not yielded even one apparent healing, he referred me to what he called an irrefutable miracle—the case of Rev. Pat Wiggins.

Mr. Wiggins, a Pentecostal evangelist whom I interviewed, told me the following story:

"I was healed of multiple sclerosis and an incurable blood disease in an Oral Roberts service. The facts of my case are thoroughly documented.

"In 1945 I developed polycythemia vera, a very rare blood condition for which medical science knows no cure. Then I became a victim of multiple sclerosis. It is the dreadful, paralyzing, crippling disease that starts in the nervous system and spreads until it affects all parts of the body.

"On February 17, 1960, God healed me through the prayers of Oral Roberts. It was in Orlando, Florida. When Brother Roberts came to me in the invalids' tent, he looked straight into my eyes. Those piercing blue eyes of his seemed to bore a hole right through me. It seemed that a flicker of recognition passed over his face but quickly disappeared. He hadn't seen me in years and he had never seen me like this—a ninety-two-pound wreck in a wheel chair.

"Then his hand shot out and was placed on my forehead. He said, 'Pat Wiggins, in the name of Jesus Christ of Nazareth, be thou made every whit whole!'

"I was able to release my faith and get up out of that wheel chair and walk.

"Some people have tried to tell me that my healing is only temporary, that I had been hypnotized at the Oral Roberts meeting and would soon come to. But I knew the doctors had tried to hypnotize me at the hospital and I hadn't been able to move my paralyzed legs an inch, much less stand up and walk.

"One doctor said to me, 'You think you're healed, but one day you're going to be walking down the street and fall flat on your face, dead.'

"That may be true, I answered, but if I do it'll be from a heart attack. I don't expect to die from the polycythemia vera or multiple sclerosis of which God has healed me."

Mr. Wiggins supported his story with documentation. He showed me photostats of letters from the Veterans' Administration offices in Washington, D.C., and St. Petersburg, Florida. The first letter, dated August 8, 1958, cited a file reference number and was addressed to Mr. Patrick Z. Wiggins, P.O. Box 4157, Chevy Chase, Maryland.

The letter read, in part: "The evidence of record shows that you are permanently and totally disabled by reason of all your disabilities."

A second letter from the same source, dated July 27, 1960, mentioned specifically "multiple sclerosis."

As part of my investigation, I talked by phone with the neurologist in Orlando, Florida, who had treated Rev. Pat Wiggins. Because of medical ethics, the doctor, a staff member of a large hospital, wished to remain anonymous.

He said that he knew Mr. Wiggins well and had great admiration for him. The doctor also mentioned that as a Seventh Day Adventist he personally believed in the possibility of miraculous healings.

"However, I want to be as truthful as I can about this case," he said. "Mr. Wiggins had a very complex case which fitted into the general multiple sclerosis category but was not a classic case of the disease. It had atypical features.

"I will say that I was impressed by his improvement. I did not expect what happened to him to happen.

"But my total impression is that this was more of a psychiatric type of cure than anything. It is not in the category of a true miracle."

My most distasteful experience with a self-styled healer concerned A. A. Allen. In August 1966, this entrepreneur of miracles came to Leaside Community Arena in metropolitan Toronto. That auditorium, which was used to the shouts of hockey fans, resounded for a week with shrieks and sobs, cries of "Glory to God," outbursts in unknown tongues, rhythmic hand-clapping, foot-stomping, and other peculiarly vociferous manifestations of what some are pleased to call "that old-time religion."

"God's Man of Faith and Power," as Allen describes himself in his advertising, announced that he was running a "miracle revival" complete with "Sight for the Blind! Hearing for the Deaf! Power to Get Wealth!" and the ability "To Cast Out Demons!"

Asa Alonzo Allen, fifty-seven, claims to have a following of "millions" as a result of his revival crusades around the world and his radio and television programs, which are carried by more than eighty stations in the United States.

He is a free-lance evangelist, ordained by himself (he heads a legal corporation, "A. A. Allen Revivals, Inc."), and shunned by many major Pentecostal groups.

The hot gospel Allen preaches is his own brand of unreconstructed Pentecostalism with an exotic admixture of visions, heavenly voices, prophecies, and such miracles as "supernatural oil" which is said to drip at times from the evangelist's hands. Allen majors in exorcism of demons ("They cause sickness," he warns, "and fear, mental illness, nervous breakdowns, and lust. . . . Eight out of ten people are domineered by demons!").

He even sells a record which purportedly captures the sounds of a demon-possessed woman. One of his books contains "eighteen pictures of demons as seen and drawn by a demon-possessed, insane person." These pictures—

images from a nightmare drawn by a schizophrenic artist with no talent—have to be seen to be believed.

Allen also lays hands on the sick for healing ("The greatest miracles of our time occur in this ministry," trumpets his advertising), and in addition mails out "blessed" handkerchiefs, or pieces of his old revival tent, which are said to bring health and prosperity to those who receive them. An advertisement in Allen's *Miracle* magazine asks for pledges of $100, $200, or $1,000 for "a prosperity cloth cut from the Old White Miracle Tent."

Another advertisment in the same magazine assures the reader that through faith he can get anything he wants from God by clipping a coupon and sending it, with a donation, to "Brother Allen for prayer in my behalf." A story in another issue of the magazine reports that "miracle sand" from Arizona has been sent around the world and that "God used it for many miracles." The sand was scooped up from a part of A. A. Allen's revival tent, runs the story, "where several people saw Jesus walking."

A typical A. A. Allen meeting in Toronto opened with a sales pitch, delivered by one of the associate evangelists, for the great man's books. Then Allen himself took over. A short, jowly man, whose face in repose hardens into a scowl, he used a hand microphone to prowl the platform, one moment roaring at the top of his lungs, the next whispering.

"Let's get lost in God tonight!" he expostulated. "We're going to de-horn the devil! I'm Pentecostal from the top of my head to the bottom of my feet and if there's one hair in my head that's not, I'll pull it out!"

Intermittently he hopped up and down, grabbed a tambourine and pounded it, or did a wild, undulating dance the length of the platform and back. A girl in the congregation threw herself into the aisle, performing cart-wheels and emitting penetrating screams. A young man, his body shaken by spasticlike contortions, groped blindly across the front of the auditorium. A woman about fifty danced up the aisle on her toes, her eyes shut, a dreamy smile on her face.

The climax of the service came when a woman was brought forward for healing. The evangelist said that, although his prayers had performed astounding miracles in the past (he cited routine healings of cancer, total blind-ness, and hermaphroditism, or as he called it, "double sexedness"), the case before him was his hardest yet.

The candidate for a miracle, a woman over fifty in a wheel chair, was said by Allen to have been a cripple for fourteen years as the result of a car accident. The evan-gelist told her: "When I lay my hands on you, you're going to feel the power of God go right through you."

He clapped his hands on her head and roared at the top of his lungs: "Walk! Walk! Walk! In Jesus' name, I *command* you to walk!"

The woman seemed to be cowed by the thunderous shouts and the evangelist's withering stare; she drew back into the wheel chair.

"Walk! In Jesus' name, walk!" he bellowed again.

This time, assisted by two ushers on either side of her who grasped her firmly by the arms and heaved, the woman tottered to her feet for a few seconds, swayed, and fell back into the wheel chair.

The evangelist solemnly told the congregation that even though the woman was miraculously healed, her muscles had wasted from disuse and would need time to function again—an announcement the people greeted with hosan-nas and hallelujahs. He asked the woman if she had faith that she was healed. She faintly nodded Yes. Then she was wheeled out of the auditorium. I tried to speak with the woman but was intercepted by one of Allen's associate evangelists, a husky young man who was adamant in refusing to let me pass. Thus I missed my opportunity to interview the greatest miracle of A. A. Allen's career.

Or perhaps his greatest miracle is surmounting his checkered past.

In 1956, A. A. Allen was disfellowshiped, defrocked—in traditional ecclesiastical terminology—by the Assemblies of God, the largest Pentecostal denomination in the United States, for "conduct unbecoming a minister." This was confirmed to me by the office of Rev. Thomas Zimmerman, General Secretary of the Assemblies of God, with headquarters in Springfield, Missouri.

Allen's expulsion was based on the fact that he jumped bail on a drunken driving charge which was laid against him in Knoxville, Tennessee, in December 1955. A spokesman for the clerk's office of the Knox County Criminal Court, Knoxville, Tennessee, said the charge against Allen was No. GSC-A 12322 in their files.

"Allen was arrested by the state highway patrol on a charge of driving while under the influence of an intoxicant," the spokesman said, "which is our legal terminology for drunk driving. The case did not come to trial because Allen failed to appear, forfeited his $1,000 bail, and left the state. If he ever enters Tennessee again he can be arrested and tried on the charge."

Needless to say, A. A. Allen has another explanation of why he is no longer an ordained minister of the Assemblies of God and why his meetings are boycotted by reputable Pentecostal churches (as was his Miami crusade in February 1965).

"I resigned from the denomination before they could ask me to leave," he says in his *Miracle* magazine. "With revival breaking out across the country as it is these days, it is evident that the devil is mad! You can't believe everything some jealous preachers say!"

An amusing postscript to the Toronto miracle revival: A. A. Allen failed to appear at the climactic final meeting of this crusade, which took place the day after his past was revealed in *The Toronto Daily Star*. His associate evangelist did put in an appearance, however, to take a collection and explain to the congregation that the Lord suddenly had called Brother Allen back to Arizona on urgent business.

My experiences with faith healers before I investigated Kathryn Kuhlman's ministry were not all negative. I was deeply impressed by my friend Rev. Alex Holmes, now minister of the Presbyterian church in Caro, Michigan, and formerly one of his native Britain's foremost exponents of prayer therapy. My book *The Unexplained* (New York, The New American Library, 1967), contains a detailed report of Holmes' ministry, including an account of the healing of Dr. Henry Smith Lieper, former Associate General Secretary of the World Council of Churches, one of the most important posts in Protestantism. Dr. Lieper suffered from an eye disorder, diagnosed as incurable by several clinics, that was corrected when he received the laying on of hands from Alex Holmes.

Another memorable experience with spiritual healing concerned a woman with crippling rheumatoid arthritis. Gertrude Geddes was a friend of my wife's and mine when we lived in Collingwood, an Ontario ship-building and resort town. She gave me a statement describing her experience in her own words.

"In the early fall of 1955 I developed a painful swelling of one hand. Rapidly, it spread into the joints of my arms, knees, ankles, and feet. In a few weeks, I was almost a total invalid.

"My niece, who came to stay with me, had to wash and even feed me. I was helpless. The doctor, who called my disease rheumatoid arthritis, prescribed various remedies. I responded to none of them. He said he doubted that I would ever be able to work again.

"A few days after Christmas my minister called on me. He was shocked at my condition. I was in pitiable shape, and in such a depression that I had almost lost the will to live. But as the minister talked with me, read the Bible, and prayed, a light went on inside me. My faith revived. For the first time in months I had hope again.

"The next time the minister called, I said: 'I've been thinking about my sickness. I don't believe God sent it— but He allowed it. Maybe He's been trying to teach me something through it. However, I've come to believe that if you pray with me and for me, I can be healed.'

"The minister said that because of my faith, not his own, he would pray for my healing. As he prayed—a simple prayer—I suddenly felt like the woman in the Gospel who reached out and touched the hem of Christ's robe and was healed. Deep within me, I knew something had happened, although my only physical sensation was a sudden sharp pain and a feeling of weakness.

"By the next morning a marvelous change was obvious. I called in my niece and showed her my hands. The terrible swelling had gone down by half. Within a few days I was downtown shopping. My niece could hardly believe the change that had taken place. My friends were astonished.

"The arthritis was completely gone and has not re-turned.

"When I walked into my doctor's office a few days after my recovery, he almost fell off his chair.

"My God, woman," he said, "what's happened to you?"
I replied, "Exactly what you said, doctor—my God."

My wife and I can vouch for what happened to Gertrude
Geddes, and it was remarkable. Indeed, in some respects
her recovery seemed even more extraordinary than this account conveys. For one thing, her hands, we remember,
were swollen into great lumps, the size (or so it seemed)
of golf balls. One thumb, in particular, was a sight to be-
hold—a deep purple color, as though it were gangrenous,
and the other fingers were gnarled. Her condition, especially in view of her previous active life, was as pathetic
as she describes it.

A significant feature is what precisely happened to her
when she was prayed for by her minister. She told us that
she felt a sudden jab of pain, like a knife going through
her, and then such a profound weakness that she thought
she was fainting. Now, as it happens, a sudden burst of
pain frequently is a sign that healing has begun. At least,
this turns up again and again in accounts of healing.

However, wonderful as this case is, it could never be
put forward as a valid miracle. Rheumatoid arthritis is
believed by many medical authorities to be a classic psychosomatic disorder—that is, one rooted in psychological
factors which are externalized in the body—and a remission of such a disease, although unusual, is not phenomenal. Psychosomatic disorders, by their very nature, may
remit suddenly, especially under the stimulus of powerful
emotion, such as religious fervor.

Nevertheless, rapid and total remissions of severe rheumatoid arthritis, like the one Miss Geddes experienced, are
not exactly everyday occurrences. If her recovery was due
merely to suggestion, as some might contend, one wonders
why doctors are not using the power of suggestion routinely

in the treatment of arthritis and producing such remissions wholesale.

Having seen Gertrude Geddes before and after her sudden and unexpected recovery—one, moreover, which took place in her own home without benefit of mass emotionalism, chanting choirs, or the exhortations of a revivalist—I was ready to accept that there is more to faith healing than most doctors seemed prepared to grant.

This conviction was consolidated during a week-long visit to Lourdes in 1965. The famous Roman Catholic shrine is in a picturesque town of about ten thousand inhabitants tucked away in the foothills of the Pyrenees in southern France.

My hostess there was Mrs. Winnifred Feely, an English-born translator with the Lourdes Medical Bureau. In 1950, when she first arrived in Lourdes, Mrs. Feely was dying from what had been diagnosed as an inoperable malignancy located between her pulmonary artery and her heart. She had, according to her doctors, six months to live.

"I came to Lourdes not primarily for physical healing," she told me, "but with the prayer, Lord let me do something for someone else before I die."

Mrs. Feely joined the army of Lourdes volunteers who help care for the sick. Since an estimated two million pilgrims a year flock to Lourdes—many of them desperately ill—helpers are always needed.

Like most pilgrims, Mrs. Feely bathed in the icy Lourdes water that flows from an underground spring. She got nothing but a chill. The next day she bathed again.

"This time my growth disappeared instantly," she said, matter-of-factly. "The X rays here at the Medical Bureau prove it. I've been at Lourdes ever since, doing my bit to help."

Was her healing a freakish case?

One might say so, if what happened to Winnifred Feely were unique. But it is not.

In the 110 years since the French peasant girl Bernadette Soubirous (now Ste. Bernadette) saw her celebrated visions of the one she called "The Lady," there have been thousands of claimed healings at Lourdes. Only sixty-four cases have been officially proclaimed by the Roman Catholic Church as canonical miracles. However, there have been thousands—yes, thousands—of other cures pronounced scientifically inexplicable by the Medical Bureau. For various technical reasons, these have not been certified as miracles.

Mrs. Feely said that during the six months immediately preceding my visit, about sixty Lourdes cures had been reported. Some, she added, were remarkable even for a place where the extraordinary tends to be ordinary.

One case concerned a twenty-three-year-old Rhodesian who was afflicted with osteosarcoma, a vicious form of cancer which had destroyed most of his hip bone. Mrs. Feely pointed to an X ray on the wall.

"This shows that his hip was just a pulpy mass," she said, in her detached, ever-so-slightly-British voice. "He was, of course, a total cripple."

While praying in the grotto at Lourdes the man was instantly healed.

"He was examined by our doctors the same day," said Mrs. Feely.

She pointed to another X ray on the wall. "This was taken a few hours after his healing. It shows that he had received a complete reconstitution of the hip bone. There is no trace of cancer. It's impossible, of course, but it happened."

The kind of healings reported at Lourdes stagger the

imagination (in fact, I was not to meet their like until my investigation of Kathryn Kuhlman's ministry). Besides cancer in various forms, there have been healings of blindness, deafness, mental retardation, organic paralysis, tuberculosis, and many other diseases. Each cure is the subject of a dossier in the files of the Lourdes Medical Bureau.

The Bureau describes itself as "a medical office officially charged to proceed with the examination of cases of cure on the day when they occur at Lourdes, and to note those cures which could not be the result of the forces of nature." No cure is accepted until it has stood the test of time. Normally three years must elapse before a cure is considered permanent.

Any doctor is free to visit the Medical Bureau, examine its records, and even take part in interviewing a person who claims a cure. Between April and October 1965, more than sixteen hundred doctors from thirty-two countries visited Lourdes and registered at the Bureau. These included Catholics, Protestants, Jews, Muslims, Hindus, and assorted freethinkers.

"The Medical Bureau," said Mrs. Feely, "is the only building in Lourdes where the word religion is not mentioned. Here, only medical facts count."

Are the healings at Lourdes actually beyond medical explanation?

The answer, it seems to me, has to be Yes.

Unless one is prepared to argue that there is a wholesale conspiracy to defraud the public—a conspiracy which includes not only leading Catholic clerics but prominent doctors from many countries, many of them non-Catholic —the evidence must be accepted as conclusive. Phenomenal cures do occur at Lourdes.

What produces these cures?

The Catholic teaching is that they are supernatural

"favors" or "graces" bestowed by Our Lady of Lourdes, the Virgin Mary. But other theories have been put forward.

There always has been talk of "suggestion," "mass hypnosis," "hysteria." Other critics, like Dr. Leslie Weatherhead, the noted British Methodist clergyman-psychologist, tend to attribute the Lourdes cures to the "spiritual atmosphere" created by the faith and prayers of millions of pilgrims. If that atmosphere were re-created elsewhere, said Dr. Weatherhead, similar cures would follow.

The late Dr. Smiley Blanton, a New York psychoanalyst, interpreted the cures in terms of a Freudian transference to the powerful symbol of the Virgin Mother.

"It is my feeling," Dr. Blanton said, "that at Lourdes there is a phenomenal quickening of the healing process (due to the emotions aroused by the transference to the all-powerful, all-loving Virgin Mother) to an extent which has not yet been realized or accepted by the medical profession."

Mrs. Feely scorned such explanations.

She pointed out that many persons have been cured at Lourdes who confessed to having no faith at all. Others were in a coma from the time they arrived at the shrine until they were cured (ah yes, but the unconscious mind never sleeps, Dr. Blanton might have said). Even infants have been healed. These cases are among the most impressive. Can an infant exercise faith, or be involved in a Freudian transference process (possibly, the psychoanalyst might reply)?

The Catholic faithful generally believe (although faith in any particular shrine is not demanded by the Church) that in February 1858, Bernadette Soubirous, a fourteen-year-old farmer's daughter, saw a vision of "The Lady" while praying in the grotto at Lourdes (there was, of course, no shrine there then). The apparition appeared to Bernadette eighteen times. The Lady gave instructions that a church was to be built on the spot and today a huge sanctuary stands atop the grotto. On another occasion, the apparition told Bernadette to dig in the ground inside the grotto. Instantly a spring gushed forth which has been flowing ever since at the rate of 27,000 gallons of water a day. Millions have bathed in it.

Lourdes is a special place. I felt it watching the crowds of pilgrims streaming to the grotto to pray. I sensed it during the torchlight procession at night in which ten thousand marchers chanted the Lourdes hymn: "Ave, Ave, Ave Maria . . ." It was this scene that came back to me during the Kathryn Kuhlman miracle service; the spirited and moving hymn-singing stirred echoes of this shrine of Lourdes, so different from the miracle service, yet so much the same.

Impressive as some of the Lourdes healings are, however, I became aware that even these were not absolutely invulnerable to medical attack. A friendly critic, British psychiatrist Donald J. West, made a careful study of eleven Lourdes "miracles" and succeeded in raising questions about them all, mainly on the grounds of faulty or insufficient documentation. He did not, however, dispute the possibility of genuinely inexplicable healings, nor that such healings do indeed happen at Lourdes.

This, then, was in part the background I brought to my investigation of the healing ministry of Kathryn Kuhlman. It was a background that contained both negative and positive experiences with faith healing. Moreover, it was one which had prompted me to scrutinize the credentials of alleged miracles, to be aware that what is commonly said to be a miracle often—in fact, nearly always—isn't.

My attitude toward inexplicable healings, then, was one of open-minded skepticism. On the evidence, I believed that such cures were possible in principle, but I was far from being persuaded that they occurred routinely, if at all, in the ministry of Kathryn Kuhlman or any other professed healer.

Little did I know or dream just how spectacular, how exciting, my results would be when I looked into the claims of Pittsburgh's auburn-haired evangelist who, in twenty years, has made that steel city a mecca of healing for thousands.

3

What Is a Miracle?

During a miracle service in Pittsburgh I saw a young woman's red, inflamed complexion visibly clear a few minutes after she received prayer from Kathryn Kuhlman.

A miracle?

No, not really. Although no doubt it seemed like one to the afflicted woman (the eczema, she said, had persisted for five years).

Medically speaking, the dramatic improvement in her complexion probably was due to temporary relief of the emotional tensions which play a large part in many skin ailments. As it happens, a psychiatrist told me of a similar remission of eczema experienced by a patient of his during a psychotherapy session.

Remarkable as it was, then, this healing would not qualify as a valid miracle. Just what sort of healing would qualify—well, that is *the* question. As we have seen, one man's miracle could apparently be another man's psychologically induced remission.

A serious researcher must find and apply rigorous objective criteria which establish that a healing is truly medically inexplicable.

What are the criteria of a miracle?

By way of caution, let's look at what may pass for a miracle with the unwary.

In the first place, some diseases are known to undergo spontaneous remissions—the sudden, usually temporary, disappearance of symptoms. Multiple sclerosis is such a disease. Normally it does not follow a relentless course but fluctuates between periods of improvement and decline.

If such a natural remission coincided with a visit to a faith healer, it might be mistaken for a miracle.

Moreover, the study of psychosomatics has established that a wide range of diseases are the expression of emotional or psychological causes. In other words, they stem not from germs or trauma (injury) but from emotional conflicts—although "accident proneness" is recognized as an aspect of psychosomatic medicine, even an injury may be unconsciously caused by an individual's will to be sick.

Since psychosomatic disorders are a kind of shadow thrown on the body by the mind, a change of mind may disperse them. Such illnesses are sometimes susceptible to sudden, dramatic improvements prompted by deep emotion.

Psychosomatic diseases and symptoms run a fantastically long gamut. One physician proposes the following partial list: asthma, sore throat, sinusitis, stammering, headache, backache, tender spine, fainting attacks, goitre, spasmodic sneezing, aphonia (loss of voice), hiccough, rapid respiration, hay fever, constipation, diarrhea, indigestion, colitis, stomach ulcer, diabetes, disturbances of urination, menstrual disorders, and nutritional diseases of the skin, teeth, and hair.

The really confusing feature of psychosomatic disorders is that they may simulate diseases which can be caused by bacterial and viral infection, or trauma. Moreover, to confound the confusion, a disease complex may have both organic and psychogenic components—-either a basic organic condition with a psychogenic overlay, as it were, or vice versa.

The common cold is a case in point. There may be, on the basis of the evidence, as many different kinds of colds as there are sufferers; in other words, a cold is anything but common.

A virologist, Dr. Robert J. Heubner, carried out research into the causes of the cold for the United States Public Health Service. In reporting his findings Dr. Heubner said: "Emotional factors may be as potent as a virus in causing the common cold." He pointed out that volunteers he had tested got equally severe cold symptoms regardless of whether they received nose drops containing viruses or drops of harmless, virus-free material. He went on to report: "Psychological tests showed a rather significant association of high gullibility scores with complaints of upper respiratory illness. Our findings indicate that susceptibility to suggestion represents a more powerful inciter to 'runny' noses than any virus we have yet discovered."

Dr. Heubner noted that a large ratio of workers piles up absenteeism laid to colds. Also, colds are most common on Monday mornings.

"Perhaps there is a Monday-morning virus," he said, "but I doubt that it could be grown even with modern tissue cultures or that miracle drugs could cure it."

A Toronto psychiatrist, Dr. Daniel Cappon, has speculated that "common colds can serve as vents for pent-up emotions. And psychiatric interviews sometimes can avoid them."

As reported in *The Toronto Daily Star,* Dr. Cappon said: "The physiologists have failed to investigate crying and laughing. I suspect there are many ways in which the body cries when the usual channel is blocked. The weeping cold is one of them."

Dr. Cappon said he sometimes encountered cases where patients could not feel with or for other people, nor could the patients express emotion in tears. Depression, for them, would break out in weeping eczema, or, if the intensity of emotion was less, in weeping colds. He reported that a psychiatric session which brought on a flood of tears often would abort a cold.

"The major factor in a cold is the attitude to illness," Dr. Cappon was reported as saying, "especially the excessive awareness of symptoms and hence psychic feedbacks of anxiety to nasal passages."

Some diseases, widely regarded as being in whole or at least in part psychosomatic, are devastating; rheumatoid arthritis is one of these.

In a press report of June 24, 1957, Dr. Sanford Gifford and Dr. Theodore B. Bayles of Boston, authorities on arthritic disorders, said: "The similarities between rheumatoid arthritis and other psychosomatic disorders are more important than any differences which can be demonstrated."

They described the typical sufferer from rheumatoid arthritis in these terms: "The patient emphasizes the mother's strength and control. Often the mother has difficulty in permitting the child to leave home or to marry. Many patients felt guilty and believed that arthritis was self-inflicted punishment for past errors. Others were trying to compensate for the loss of a loved one."

Interestingly, the worst case of crippling arthritis which I have seen involved an elderly man of extremely conservative and rigid religious views, who told me that his suffering was a penalty sent by God for the sins of his youth. One got the impression that he would have considered any serious effort to get well as virtual impiety.

Another severe disorder, which has uncountable victims and can cause acute misery, is allergic (so-called) eczema —and it, too, appears to be, at least in some cases, psychogenic. Dr. William B. Guy and Dr. Robert J. Shoemaker of the University of Pittsburgh reported in 1957 that in extreme froms this disorder "is as crippling as paralytic polio, muscular dystrophy, or rheumatoid arthritis." They traced allergic eczema not to an allergen at all but to a particular skin chemistry that is sensitive to emotional frustrations plus the emotional makeup that leads to the skin reactions. (Amazing remissions of chronic eczema can sometimes be provoked by encouraging the patient to tell off his spouse, or in-laws, say, the doctors reported.) The skin lesions appeared to be related to the inability to express even justified anger or annoyance.

This is not a treatise on psychosomatic medicine, but, since it is important that we know how to distinguish a miracle from a psychosomatic remission, let's consider a few further illustrations of the mind's ability to hex the body.

Tuberculosis is an example of a disease with an undeniable bacterial cause which may have important psychosomatic concomitants. Of the countless individuals who are unwitting hosts to the tubercle bacillus—the causative organism in TB—some stay healthy while others fall sick, often gravely. Why the difference? Obvious possible reasons suggest themselves: nutrition, housing, hygiene. But these appear to be only partial answers at best.

A seven-year study of fifteen hundred tuberculosis patients by Seattle psychiatrist Thomas H. Holmes yielded new evidence that TB is triggered by emotional factors. Paralleling a similar British study, the findings showed that more than half of the victims in the study group came from homes disrupted by death, or a divorce or separation of the parents, before the patients were eighteen. The divorce rate among the tuberculous themselves was four times the national average. The TB patients also had more than their statistical share of emotional illness: 36 percent had overt neuroses.

Dr. Holmes and his associates in the study concluded that the tuberculosis victims were not at ease in their environment and their frantic strivings to adjust led to cumulative emotional conflict, anxiety, frustration, and depression. The TB broke out, apparently, when their limited capacities were no longer adequate to resolve their problems.

Now, such findings would have to be taken into account in evaluating any healing of tuberculosis by a faith healer. Did the healer merely strengthen the patient's ability to face life and cope with his problems? Even if this were so, the cure might have genuinely unexplained elements, however.

For example, if the patient had sustained massive lung cavities and these closed much more rapidly than normal, that could constitute an inexplicable feature of what otherwise might be called "merely" a psychosomatic recovery. A "psychosomatic" occurrence does not necessarily preclude a "miraculous" one.

Before concluding this summary of some of the guises in which psychosomatic disease disports itself, I would like to note that a cause-and-effect relationship—although a remote one—can be established between cancer and the emotions. And since, as Robert Southey said, "what thought can cause, another thought can cure," presumably cancer provoked by unhealthy thought habits could respond to a change in those habits.

It is a medical fact that a stomach ulcer is a classic, emotionally-induced disorder, typically brought on by the kind of tension that "eats at" an individual. Something, literally, is eating him. And, in a few cases, stomach ulcers become cancerous. Whether or not the patients would have developed cancer without the ulcers is moot, but the transition from the stomach ulcer, a psychosomatic disease, to cancer has been established.

Psychiatrist L. Gilbert Little has described how a typical case of stomach ulcer developed.

The patient, a plant manager, lived in constant fear that he would be by-passed for promotion in favor of someone else. What he feared did happen and his stomach, which had been giving him trouble, presented him with a full-blown ulcer. An operation was performed severing the nerves leading from the stomach to the brain, the purpose being to prevent the impulses of anger, resentment, rage, and frustration, which were being generated in the patient's brain, from reaching his stomach and inflaming the ulcer.

As a result of the surgery the ulcer symptoms subsided. However, the patient continued to seethe with negative emotions. Eventually these broke out in other overt symptoms—a complete nervous breakdown with physical paralysis.

This case illustrates another characteristic of psychosomatic symptoms—if one set is repressed or removed (by a faith healer, suggestion, or some other means), another may emerge to take its place. It is as though the underlying emotional conflict demands expression and, deprived of one outlet, fights its way into the open by a different route.

It is possible, therefore, that a person at a faith-healing

meeting may simply exchange one set of psychosomatic symptoms for another. And his second state may be—although this is by no means certain—worse than the first.

Another important distinction is between genuinely organic disorders and their hysterical impersonations.

The word hysteria in this context does not mean an emotional outburst characterized by weeping and wailing. In the medical, or psychiatric, sense hysteria is a psychological condition in which disease symptoms which appear to be rooted in organic, physical causes are actually rooted in purely emotional ones. Psychiatrists speak of "conversion hysteria" in which an emotional trauma is translated—converted—into physical symptoms, sometimes of a devastating nature.

Hysterical symptoms are a form of psychosomatic disease—or, if you prefer, psychosomatic disease is a form of hysteria—but probably it is better to distinguish between the two. Generally speaking, in a proper psychosomatic disorder such as asthma or atopic eczema, the basic cause may indeed be emotional, but normally it is a state of mind or attitude rather than a single traumatic experience. Also, there probably are contributing factors which are physical —infection, allergy, heredity—and often the disease involves actual tissue damage or other detectable physical changes. Moreover, this kind of psychosomatic condition is unlikely to yield suddenly and dramatically to one therapeutic session or approach.

On the other hand, in the case of what we may call here true hysteria, the physical condition often is a single symptom—blindness, deafness, paralysis of an arm, tremors similar to those produced by palsy—which may disappear instantly if the causative trauma, typically a single event, is isolated and dispersed as, for example, by psychotherapy. In hysteria, the condition is wholly due to emotion with, typically, no organic changes involved. Thus, in hysterical blindness the eyes are perfectly normal, but the victim still cannot see.

Psychologist F. L. Marcuse describes a hysterical symptom which was relieved by hypnotherapy.[1] The case, as Marcuse reports it, concerns a seaman who had been torpedoed during World War II.

He had an uncontrollable muscular motion in his arm for which he could give no plausible reason and which had developed shortly after his ship was sunk. The sailor had been blown on deck from below, and to give vent to his rage at the aerial attack had searched for a machine gun to fire back but could not find one. The muscular action of his arm was precisely the motion that would have been involved in firing the machine gun.

Marcuse says the seaman, under hypnosis, was encouraged to relive the incident and did so, with great discharge of emotion. When he awakened, the uncontrollable tremor in his arm had ceased.

An account of how a hysterical condition was developed experimentally is provided by Dr. Lewis Wolberg, a New York psychiatrist, in the journal, *Psychosomatic Medicine*, September–October, 1947. He inducted a patient into a deep hypnotic trance and gave him the suggestion that when he awakened he would find a chocolate bar next to him and have an irresistible desire to eat it. However, at the same time he would feel that since the chocolate did not belong to him, to eat it would be very wrong.

When the subject was awakened, there was a visible conflict between his overpowering urge to eat the chocolate and his feeling that it would be wrong to do so. The internal struggle was prolonged. The patient eventually be-

[1] F. L. Marcuse, *Hypnosis, Fact and Fiction* Pelican Books, Baltimore, Md., 1959.

came faint, grew pale, and had to be assisted to a chair to rest. His forehead was bathed in perspiration and he complained of chills. When his pulse was taken, it proved to be abnormally rapid. At length, he started to shake with severe muscular tremors which became more violent whenever he turned his head toward the chocolate. Finally, he seemed to lapse into a faint. His distress vanished instantly when he was rehypnotized and the original suggestions were removed.

Significantly, the physical symptoms evoked by this experimental neurosis were markedly similar to those of influenza.

In a like experiment by Dr. Wolberg, the results were slightly but significantly different. The patient, in this case, finally ate the desired but forbidden chocolate. However, very shortly after, he became nauseated and disgorged it, illustrating that his unconscious had seized on a shrewd compromise—he both ate the candy and he didn't.

These experiments show how the mind can convert a deep but unconscious impulse into physical symptoms that impersonate organic disease.

A man may be stone blind—yet have nothing whatsoever wrong with him physically. There have been cases of hysterical blindness in war when soldiers used this means of blotting out an experience they found intolerable. Or they developed hysterical paralysis as a means of getting invalided out of the battle zone.

There are even recognized, standard hysterical counterparts of some diseases, so common that they have a special name. One of these is hystero-epilepsy, which masquerades as the real thing, but is caused not by a brain abnormality but emotional trauma.

The relevance of hysterical disorders to faith healing is evident. If a believer with hysterical lameness, say, were commanded by a revivalist to get up from his wheel chair and walk he probably would, to cries of hallelujah from the crowd.

It should be realized, too, that the body can be stimulated to abnormal performance by powerful emotion. In a fire, cripples have been known to run from the hospital, and collapse. This is similar to a mother lifting an automobile to free her trapped child. Incidents of such hyper-adrenal performance have been credibly reported.

The miracle hunter should be fully aware of the huge but often underestimated power of suggestion.

A vivid example of suggestion as therapy is found in the career of Emile Coué, the French pharmacist who in the 1920s popularized the litany, "Every day in every way I'm getting better." Coué operated a clinic at Nancy, France, and students from all over the world flocked to learn his technique of stimulating health by autosuggestion.

Coué's method, which was psychologically sound, was to repeat to oneself, rapidly, twenty times, morning and night, the formula quoted above: "Every day in every way . . ." The best time, said Coué, was just before falling asleep and immediately upon awakening, for the mind is then in a kind of twilight (actually, hypnoidal) state which makes it readily susceptible to suggestion.

During a lecture tour of the United States, Coué drew crowds to his meetings at which he described and demonstrated his technique. Newspaper accounts of some of these meetings make them sound like present-day revival services. The only features lacking were hymn-singing and the collection (that already had been taken at the door).

In one meeting Coué demonstrated his method with several cripples. His first two tries were unsuccessful, but he had more luck with his third case, a man who said he had been on crutches for years. Rubbing the crippled leg rhythmically, Coué intoned his magical formula, "Ce passe, ce passe" ("It is going, it is going"). The man said that feeling was coming back into his leg, and presently he was able to walk across the stage, to the applause and cheers of the audience.

No one, of course, knows what the cause of his lameness was, or his eventual condition. But no doubt some present were sure they had witnessed a genuine miracle. Maybe it was a miracle of a sort, but probably not the sort I was looking for.

The "placebo effect" so well known to doctors is pure suggestion. A placebo is "dummy" medication given to a patient who thinks he is getting the genuine thing. Some patients respond as well to a placebo as to real medication; a sugar pill may relieve pain, for example, as effectively as morphine.

It seems hard to exaggerate the importance of this placebo effect in view of an article in the *Journal of the American Medical Association,* March 21, 1966. This summarized the results of a five-year study on children with hay fever, attributed to sensitivity to ragweed. A comparison was made of symptom relief obtained from specific hyposensitization injections—the most common treatment for this disease—and placebo injections consisting of sterile water.

The conclusions of the medical investigators: "Even though the allergen injections may have had some beneficial effect on some children, the amount of benefit was indistinguishable from differences likely to occur in pure randomization experiments. No justification was found for promising any greater benefit to children treated with allergens than they would obtain from placebo injections."

Psychologist F. L. Marcuse, in his previously mentioned book, reports two cases in which the placebo effect overcame even the normal consequences of actual medication. A pregnant woman whose complaint was vomiting had her nausea eased when she was told that the drug she took would produce such relief. Actually she was given a substance that normally induces nausea and vomiting! In a similar case, constipation was relieved when the patient took what he believed to be a laxative but was actually a constipation-producing drug.

When you come to formal hypnosis—or direct suggestion—the ramifications are astonishingly vast. Hypnosis certainly is not magic or a panacea as some uncritical enthusiasts have claimed. But the range of physical effects it can produce is very wide.

Among others, bleeding from a wound can be inhibited; respiration can be slowed materially; pain can be relieved, or immunity to pain, either localized or general, conferred (this is called hypnothesia); some skin rashes can be relieved; blood pressure can be altered; the flow and character of gastric secretions can be influenced (a hypnotized subject will secrete pepsin, an enzyme normally present only during digestion of a meal, if he is told he is eating); a blister can be formed at a designated spot by suggesting a burn; rales—the characteristic wheezing of asthma—can be created by regressing an asthma-free subject to a period when he suffered from the disease.

Granted, however, that hypnosis can evoke a variety of somatic effects, can it relieve—cure, even—organic disorders? Can it regress cancer, say, or close a wound with phenomenal rapidity?

An indication of what the potentialities of hypnotherapy may be is in a report published by the staid *British Medical Journal* of August 1952. It concerns a case of icthyosis treated hypnotically by a London physician, Dr. Albert Abraham Mason.

Icthyosis—fish-scale disease—is a hideous ailment, usually congenital, in which the victim's skin hardens into a black, rough casing that sometimes covers most of the body. The patient treated by Dr. Mason was a sixteen-year-old boy whose whole body was affected except the chest, neck, and face. The boy had been born with the disease and attempts to treat him by grafting normal skin from his chest to the affected parts proved useless. The skin grafts rapidly turned black and rough like the rest.

Dr. Mason decided to try hypnosis. In a hospital in East Grinstead, Sussex, he put the boy into a trance while a dozen skeptical doctors watched. It took ten minutes. Then Mason said again and again: "Your left arm will clear." The idea of starting with a particular part of the body was to focus the suggestion and make the test more precise.

About five days later the coarse outer layer on the boy's left arm became soft and crumbly and flaked off. The skin underneath was pink and soft. In ten days the whole arm was clear.

Gradually, in response to repeated suggestions, the parts of his body affected by the icthyosis became 90 percent clear. The boy, jubilant, learned self-hypnosis to maintain the improvement.

This case is peculiarly impressive because of the nature of the illness. Since icthyosis is congenital, it cannot, by conventional norms, be considered psychosomatic. Though the cause of the disease is unknown, it could not be presumably emotional conflict in an unborn child (unless prenatal traumata are possible, as a few psychoanalysts believe, and such traumata can exteriorize themselves on the body of the fetus—an idea, at present, extremely speculative; for more information see *Search for the Beloved*, New York: Hermitage Press, 1949, by Nandor Fodor).

However, it should be noted that the remission of the

icthyosis was partial, gradual, and also temporary (temporary in the sense that hypnotic treatment had to be continued, apparently, to maintain the improvement). By contrast, the best cases of healing at Lourdes appear to have been complete, quasi-instantaneous (or at least very rapid) and permanent.

Some criteria for a miracle were emerging in my mind as I pursued studies such as the above. Such a healing, ideally, should have the following features:

1. The disease should be a medically diagnosed organic or structural disorder.

2. The healing should be rapid, preferably quasi-instantaneous, and involve changes of a type not normally considered attributable to suggestion.

3. The healing should be permanent.

This, then, was the classic kind of healing I was looking for in Kathryn Kuhlman's ministry. And, these are the kinds of healings I found, a number of which will be described in later chapters.

Aware that most books written about alleged miraculous cures were ill-documented—in some cases not at all—I aimed for the strongest possible documentation in this book. One fairly recent book on purported miraculous healings, described in a jacket blurb as "a reporter's documented account," turned out to contain only one case in which names, dates, and places were mentioned. A large number of apparently astounding healings were referred to in the book—a woman cured of an inoperable brain tumor, a child crippled by polio who got up and walked, a bedridden tuberculosis patient who returned to work in five days after receiving prayer—but curiously no documentation of any kind was offered. One cannot help but wonder if this was because no documentation existed.

At any rate, such an approach is worse than useless because it outrages the open-minded skeptic, who is prepared to believe even the unbelievable if the evidence warrants it, but refuses to exercise a heroic faith in the veracity of an author who claims to have seen miracles but offers not a scintilla of proof.

My original goal was to achieve for each healing a level of medical documentation that was virtually airtight, leaving no room for possible dispute. However, I soon realized that this target was unrealistic and, moreover, fatuous to boot.

Let me explain. If a purported healing is supported by very strong evidence but lacks some item of technical medical data that would make the case absolutely invulnerable, it would be foolish to reject it on these grounds. Judging by the controversies that often rage within the medical fraternity itself over the merits and demerits of a particular theory or treatment, airtight documentation of claims is exceedingly rare, even among doctors. For that matter, how many reports in medical journals are infallibly documented?

It seemed to me, as I reflected on it, that testimony of intelligent, reputable but nonmedical witnesses to a healing should be accepted where it obviously was competent. If a mother, for instance, says that her baby was born with a club foot, gives a description of the deformity consonant with that diagnosis, and reports that several doctors told her repeatedly that it was a club foot, her testimony is significant. Obviously not competent to diagnose the condition herself, she is, surely, competent to know what the doctors told her about the condition.

This question of invulnerable medical documentation is clouded by the fact that doctors—even highly qualified ones—sometimes disagree on the diagnosis and prognosis of a case. In one Kathryn Kuhlman healing in which a nine-year-old boy recovered suddenly from Perthe's Disease, or aseptic necrosis of the hip, the judgment of two different doctors was contradictory. (This is a malady of unknown cause in which the bone rots, forming a cavity.) One doctor, an orthopedist, told me that such a recovery was not unusual because natural remissions sometimes occur in Perthe's Disease. But the second doctor, a radiologist, said that he had made a careful study of the case and was convinced that the boy's recovery was medically extraordinary, attributing it to Kathryn Kuhlman's ministry.

Furthermore, I discovered that between different medical specialties there can be marked disagreement about what constitutes a "classic" healing. Thus, a pathologist disapproved of any purported healings involving certain neurological disorders—such as myasthenia gravis—because these are not "anatomically detectable." Rule out such cases to begin with, he advised. (Myasthenia gravis is a chronic disease of unknown origin, but generally considered neurological in character, in which the muscles waste.)

This pathologist was impressed by the case of a woman suffering gross enlargement of the heart who experienced a total subsidence of clinical symptoms, with confirmation of the healing by laboratory tests. He urged me to emphasize such "clear-cut" cases as this.

A psychiatrist, on the other hand, was impressed by the case of myasthenia gravis—on the basis of preliminary data—and told me it would be foolish to reject it in principle. He said the pathologist was too "tissue oriented" and not sufficiently aware of the emotional role in illness. The heart healing did not especially impress this psychiatrist because, he said, pronounced improvement in cardiac cases had been known to follow an emotional crisis.

A myth that my research punctured was that of the necessary reliability of doctors as judges of what is or is not medically supernormal. In the beginning, there were times when I was tempted to be intimidated by the professional skepticism of doctors based, I was assured, on their expertise. But in some cases their skepticism proved to be less rigorous than my own. In one instance two highly qualified doctors described as "classic" a healing which I found to have imperfect features overlooked by both of them. At any rate, in the hard cases that follow, I shall not feature any in which doctors disagreed over diagnoses.

The logistics involved in checking out healings can be onerous. Besides extended visits to Pittsburgh, Youngstown, Los Angeles, and San Francisco, I had to make numerous trips to relatively out-of-the-way places. It would be tedious to narrate the number of times I had to call back, in some cases, to interview someone, the difficulties of catching busy doctors, especially, on the run.

Everyone quoted in this book in relation to a particular healing was interviewed by me, and the interviews were tape recorded.

The problems of getting formal medical documentation can be considerable. In one case, for example, the person healed had been treated by a hospital on an out-patient basis and such out-patient records were destroyed after ten years. The healing occurred eighteen years ago. In another case, the attending doctors had died.

In some instances people neglected to procure their medical records as they had promised to do. In others, repeated requests to doctors for a patient's medical records —with consent of the patient—yielded no results.

On balance, I reached the following conclusion: My goal would be to amass, for each healing, evidence sufficient to establish the case "beyond reasonable doubt" by the standards applied in a court of law. Such data would include, besides available medical documents, personal testimony of nonmedical witnesses where relevant, and possible circumstantial evidence (for instance, a corrective brace worn by the person healed which would indicate the probable nature of his affliction).

This more realistic goal—more realistic, that is, than the virtually unattainable one of technically perfect documentation—meant, of course, that some of the healings might not be absolutely unassailable. But then, there are few things in this world beyond dispute, especially in medicine. And I believe the evidence revealed in this book can be viewed as substantial, to say the least—even by skeptics.

My decision was that the testimony of one or more informed and competent medical authorities that a particular healing was inexplicable, or outside the normal course of the disease process, would be sufficient. In addition, of course, to the testimony of the people healed and/or those close to the people healed.

"Miraculous healings," a doctor once informed me, "are a logical impossibility."

I replied that I didn't care if they were impossible; the question was, Did they happen?

That reminds me of Simon Newcomb.

Some sixty-one years ago, Newcomb was one of the most important scientists in the United States. So great was his reputation as an astronomer and mathematician that he became the first American since Benjamin Franklin to be made an associate of the Institute of France.

In an article in *The Independent* magazine of October 22, 1903, Newcomb proved conclusively that flight in a heavier-than-air machine was impossible. Such flight, he said, would require the discovery of some new metal or a new unsuspected force in nature. "The demonstration that no possible combination of known substances, known forms of machinery and known forms of force, can be united in a practical machine by which men shall fly long distances through the air, seems to me as complete as it is possible for the demonstration of any physical fact to be," Newcomb wrote.

Moreover, argued the great scientist, even if a man did, by some incredible feat, get aloft, he wouldn't be able to stop without disastrous consequences.

"Once he slackens his speed," wrote Newcomb, "down he begins to fall. Once he stops, he falls a dead mass. How shall he reach the ground without destroying his delicate machinery? I do not think that even the most imaginative inventor has yet put on paper a demonstrative, successful way of meeting this difficulty."

Two months after this article appeared—that is, on December 17, 1903—Wilbur and Orville Wright made the first powered flight in the history of mankind with a heavier-than-air craft, and the air age began.

Even then, Simon Newcomb did not capitulate. At first he pooh-poohed the press reports as merely newspaper talk. Only when the Wright brothers' feat became established as an undeniable fact did he retreat—and then only by inches.

As late as September, 1908, a year before his death, Newcomb told a newspaper reporter who asked him if there would ever be passenger planes: "No, because no plane could ever carry the weight of anyone besides the pilot."

Lavoisier, the chemist who was one of the eighteenth century's outstanding men of science, refused to believe in meteorites in spite of the abundant eyewitness reports.

"It is impossible," he said, "for stones to fall from the sky."

More recently, in May 1957, Britain's Astronomer Royal Dr. Richard Woolley—holder of the most important astronomical post in the country—said, when asked if space travel was a future possibility: "Space travel is utter bilge!" These words were uttered five months before the Russians put up the first sputnik, opening the age of space travel. Today, a little more than ten years later, man has landed on the moon.

Notwithstanding, I feel impelled to say, in all fairness, that there is a place for prejudice—in the literal sense of that word, that is, prejudgment—in science. Science does not proceed, after all, by blind guesses but by constructing hypotheses or theoretical models and testing them. Facts which don't fit any theory more often than not do turn out to be erroneous. As Sir Arthur Eddington put it: "Never believe a fact unless you have a theory to support it."

However, the history of science—and in particular, medical science—is strewn with cases where brilliant men let their *a priori*s get in the way of facts. It's an old story: Semmelweis and the cause of childbed fever, Harvey and the circulation of the blood, Simpson and chloroform, Braid and medical hypnotism—all these were cases of pioneers whose discoveries were rejected and later proved valid.

Our main question is: Do miraculous healings take place?

Such a question should be decided on the basis not of theory, but of hard evidence. And the evidence is that they do happen—in Kathryn Kuhlman's meetings, for instance.

Mind you, I confess to more than a little sympathy with the doctor who fears that to acknowledge miracles is a step backward to the medical dark ages when the insane were

whipped to drive the demons out of them and animal dung
was used to poultice wounds.

It certainly is not for a return to such obscurantism that
I am arguing, but merely for an open-mindedness toward
the possibility that what can and cannot happen is a question for which we do not have all the answers.

What, precisely, *is* a "miracle"?

The dictionary offers this common definition: "In theology, an event or effect that apparently contradicts known
scientific laws and is hence thought to be due to supernatural causes . . ."

I prefer a second definition given: "A wonderful thing."

Personally (and this is my own view—one, moreover,
that is not shared by a number of the people quoted in
this book, certainly not by Kathryn Kuhlman), I think that
if miracles happen, surely they are natural phenomena.
Nothing, to me, is supernatural, only *supernormal* (beyond
the normal, the usual). "Whatever is part of nature is
natural," said Goethe. Nature I take here to mean the
totality of what is.

The idea that miracles break natural law seems
anachronistic. Of course, the definition does not say *that*;
what it does say is that a miracle "apparently contradicts
known scientific laws," which is another matter.

Moreover, what is scientific "law" today may not be
tomorrow. (Although there are certain fundamental concepts most scientists just could not conceive of as being
wrong—such as the Second Law of Thermodynamics which
rules out perpetual motion. Also called the law of entropy,
or the degradation of energy, this states that heat or energy
cannot flow from a colder to a warmer body; therefore, it
is not possible to build a machine that goes on forever
without receiving energy from an outside source.)

However, often what appears to contradict natural or scientific law may not really do so. Simon Newcomb concluded that heavier-than-air flight was impossible because it contradicted known laws. He was wrong. In point of fact, the principles of aerodynamics that enabled the Wright brothers to fly were merely a new adaption and extension of old and familiar concepts. Instead of the weight of air keeping a plane down, as Newcomb argued, it keeps a plane aloft.

To define a miracle as something that contradicts natural laws is gratuitous. Heavier-than-air flight, as we've seen, was said to contradict natural law. So was the transmutation of metals, before atomic physicists got around to making new metals from old (such as berkelium and beryllium). A miracle has often been anything you don't understand.

Let me propose an empirical, purely descriptive definition: A miracle of healing is any such phenomenon which, beyond reasonable doubt, is scientifically inexplicable.

By "scientifically inexplicable" I do not mean to suggest that an explanation is totally inconceivable, only that science at present cannot offer any proved or generally accepted explanation. Someday we may discover the natural laws which govern the straightening of twisted limbs and the remission of tumors, but today we can only speculate about them.

Let's look at a few cases of healing which seem, beyond reasonable doubt, to be scientifically inexplicable. Two are reported by a highly credible witness, Dr. Robert Hoyt, a clinical pathologist who holds two degrees from the University of California (B.A. and M.D.) and took post-doctoral studies in pathology at the University of Cambridge. In addition to his having taken further studies at the University of California at Berkeley, he is a diplomate of the American Board of Pathology. He is currently on the staff of a large San Francisco area hospital, and teaches clinical pathology on a university faculty.

"I believe this is one of the great miracles of Kathryn Kuhlman's ministry," said Dr. Hoyt.

The patient had bladder cancer. It had been medically diagnosed and was bothering him with tremendous pain and a need to pass urine every few minutes. I know about bladder cancer and it is a terrible affliction. This man was in a living hell. Sometimes, patients who cannot stand the pain and misery of this condition commit suicide.

In the Kathryn Kuhlman service this man raised his hands in the air while singing a hymn and gave his heart, his life, and his body to God to use however God wanted. He said he felt as though a hand had taken hold of his. In that moment, several things happened to him.

One, he had a great spiritual change, he got a new lease on life and purpose in living.

Two, he got completely rid of his alcoholism.

Three, he got completely rid of all pain and discomfort in his bladder and had no more symptoms from that moment on.

He went back to his doctor, a urologist, who reported that his bladder looked normal. The growth was gone.

Now, I would not use this case to prove miraculous healing because, from the strictly medical aspect, it has a weakness—the fact that the patient had had previous surgery and a lot of radiation therapy.

However, in my mind there is no doubt this was an instantaneous miracle. Not only was the man physically healed but his life—and this is what confirms it as a miracle for me—was transformed and his alcoholic problem vanished. Today that man and his wife are turned on spiritually with love for God and for other people.

Dr. Hoyt described another, somewhat similar, healing.

This is one of the most amazing—and also, unfortunately, one of the hardest to document.

A woman had a large tumor involving her uterine cervix and vagina. The diagnosis was made visually by a doctor, a gynecologist, in Los Angeles. Unfortunately, they did not do a biopsy.

This woman came to a Kathryn Kuhlman meeting and was healed. She went back to her doctor and he discovered the tumor was gone. Now, that's amazing. I can't explain this medically.

About the only way you could discredit it would be to say that the doctor didn't know what he was looking at. And, really, I can't imagine that in a case like this.

These cases were checked out by Dr. Hoyt as part of a projected documentation of Kathryn Kuhlman healings.

Another report by a doctor, in this case an eyewitness, comes from Dr. James Blackann, a physician and surgeon of Youngstown, Ohio.

"I was in a Kathryn Kuhlman miracle service in Pittsburgh," Dr. Blackann told me, "when a young boy, nine years old, was brought in who had a foot deformity. His feet were turned in to the point where he was tripping over them."

The only way they could get him to walk straight was to put steel-plated shoes on him.

This condition was congenital. Presumably while the fetus was developing the feet became turned in the uterus and stayed that way, just as with a club foot.

The child's mother had taken him to an orthopedist near Pittsburgh who told her the only way to straighten the child's legs was to do major surgery, cut the femur, turn it, pin it, and put a cast on, and the cast would have to stay on some five or six months.

The child asked his mother to bring him to the Kathryn Kuhlman meeting. They were at the back of the auditorium when Miss Kuhlman called out the healing of a child's legs and the boy said, "Mother, that's me. My legs are healed."

His mother took off the boy's shoes and he walked. The boy walked up on the stage, ran back and forth, and skipped.

I was sitting there watching closely and Miss Kuhlman said, "Dr. Blackann, would you come up here and examine this boy's legs and see if he's telling the truth?" So I examined him.

And?

"God had miraculously healed that boy's legs. They were straight, as normal as any boy's. That happened in May 1968."

Another doctor who believes in miracles is Martin Biery of Anaheim, California.

A graduate of Michigan State University (B.S.) and of the University of Michigan (M.D.), Dr. Biery most recently spent seven years as a Chief Surgeon on the staff of the U.S. Veterans' Administration Hospital in Long Beach, California.

A boy in his early twenties was at a Kathryn Kuhlman miracle service [Dr. Biery said]. He had played football in high school and as a result of injury had developed osteo-chondritis—a condition of the knee in which there is a change in the synovial lining of the joint and changes in the cartilage. The boy's symptoms were marked pain, an inability to flex the knee totally, and, of course, an inability to walk normally.

It is a very disabling condition and extremely painful. There is not much you can do in the way of treatment, except casting the knee to protect it from flexing over a long period of time.

This boy was miraculously healed in the service. I examined him and he was able to completely flex his knee, to put his full weight on it, and to bend and extend his leg fully—which he hadn't been able to do since the injury.

To me, this was just medically unexplainable.

An expert in arthritis, Dr. Biery said he was particularly interested in healings of this disease which he had seen in Kathryn Kuhlman's meetings.

> As medical consultant for the State Rehabilitation Board in Orange County, I see dozens of cases of arthritis. I've been studying the disease and lecturing on it.
>
> Arthritis is terribly crippling. In rheumatoid arthritis there is a change in the structure of the joints with swelling and deformity. And in the Marie-Strumpelles type of arthritis—they call it poker spine—the vertebrae totally freeze together. The inflammatory reaction causes the vertebrae to disintegrate and the bones literally fuse.
>
> I have seen such cases totally healed in Kathryn Kuhlman's meetings. I've examined many women on the stage during the service who were unable to bend or flex or twist and who got release. To me, this is a fantastic miracle.

It is impossible to *prove* that supernormal healings occur in Kathryn Kuhlman's meetings, just as it is impossible to *prove* anything else—outside of mathematics and logic. Science has to be satisfied with levels of probability. It is probable the sun will rise tomorrow, so probable that we consider it certain. Probability, then, in some cases reaches such a high level that it constitutes virtual proof.

Now, it seems evident that something more than mere chance is responsible for the healings in Kathryn Kuhlman's meetings. There are just too many of them for them to be random. The level of probability, therefore, is very high that some extra-chance factor is at work.

But what is this x-factor?

It is a question we will come across again and again,

and one which I will eventually discuss more fully.

Suffice it to say here that Kathryn Kuhlman believes the healing factor is the direct intervention of God. For now, I am satisfied to call it anti-chance, which is about as purely descriptive and nonphilosophical as you can get. Even a rank skeptic, I submit, would have to agree the facts justify saying that anti-chance is evident in the Kuhlman cures.

What about the limits, if any, of this healing factor?

If a bladder cancer apparently can regress out of existence, why not a massive tumor?

If cataracts can melt, what about the opposite phenomenon—the restoration of tissue?

If congenitally deformed legs can straighten instantly, could shattered and even pulverized bones be reconstituted?

If spines frozen by arthritis can be released in a few moments, why not spines grossly twisted or even mangled?

The doctors who asserted their belief in Kathryn Kuhlman's miracles offered their views about the explicit source of the healings, and its possible limits.

"To my mind, the miracles in Kathryn Kuhlman's meetings are the same as those recorded in the Book of Acts in the Bible," allowed Dr. Hoyt.

"Until two years ago I was very skeptical of purported cases of divine or spiritual healing. My father, who was a doctor and at one time president of the American Urological Association, believed that there was such a thing as miracles. But in my younger years I used to argue with him about this.

"My belief in spiritual healing started with an experience I myself had.

"I was sick with a minor illness—the flu, actually—and had been away from work when some friends came and insisted on praying for me. I must say that I was somewhat opposed to the idea but I couldn't refuse without bruising their feelings. So I sat down on a chair and they prayed for me.

"At that moment, I felt a change take place. It was a tremendous experience. I actually felt something occur in my chest.

"Well, my symptoms disappeared. I was running a fever and it was hard for me to get out of bed, but after the prayer I put on my clothes immediately and went back to work.

"This was enough to convince me that there was really something in prayer for the physical body."

Dr. Hoyt cautioned against miracle-mongering.

"I would like to emphasize that I am first of all a medical man. There is a place for medicine, and if you're sick, unless a real miracle occurs, you'd better have a doctor.

"Furthermore, no one but a medical man can say whether or not the miraculous has occurred in a healing. This is why Kathryn Kuhlman always tells people to go back to see their doctor, and probably a few others.

"For me, what makes her ministry so valid is that she welcomes at any time those with professional medical training—and, for that matter, anybody else, if they're interested—to come and examine and question people who claim a healing.

"I remember a man at a service in Los Angeles who said he had had tumors involving the subcutaneous tissue of the abdomen and that these suddenly had disappeared right in the meeting. Miss Kuhlman called on me to examine this man on the spot, which I did. Even with his shirt on, I could feel that he still had tumors and I reported this."

As a physician, said Dr. Hoyt, his attitude toward any alleged spiritual healer was one of initial skepticism.

"I am suspicious of all healers—every one of them—until I see something that proves to me there is the miraculous in their ministry."

Dr. Hoyt also cautioned against the practice of people removing casts and braces at faith-healing meetings.

"I feel very strongly about this, that one should not be removing casts from people who have had fractures because on their testimony alone you simply cannot tell if they have really been healed."

His reservation in this respect was not because of any known case of injury to a person in a Kathryn Kuhlman meeting, he added—"I've had none reported to me from her ministry"—but because of "other ministries and the problems relating to other ministries."

For him, Dr. Hoyt reaffirmed, the genuine healings in the Kuhlman services "can only be compared to the healings at the time of Christ."

Dr. Biery said that his experience leads him to believe that there are no limits to the healing power.

"I feel there is nothing God cannot do," he asserted. "It's as simple as that.

"After all, in any healing—even after medical treatment—it is the Lord who heals. My thirty years in medicine have shown me that in the human body God constructed a wonderful, a miraculous and intricate, mechanism. And the power that put our bodies together certainly can heal them.

"To me, Kathryn Kuhlman is an arm of the Lord."

Theoretically, no limits need be put on the healings possible in Kathryn Kuhlman's ministry, declared Dr. Blackann, "because there are no limitations with God, and it is God who's working through Kathryn Kuhlman.

"I've seen massive cysts disperse immediately. I've seen spastic conditions disappear. I've seen arthritic spines and limbs instantly freed in her services.

"God, you see, has no limits."

Although science, in its present form, cannot explain what happens when a tumor disappears, some medical scientists have speculated about the possible processes and mechanisms involved.

The image of the human body as a configuration of whirling electrons makes such phenomena as vanishing tumors more plausible, argues New York psychiatrist Gotthard Booth.

"The apparent solidity of matter has been proved an illusion of our sense organs," he writes.[2]

"It comes about in a manner roughly similar to the illusion of solid objects in three-dimensional moving pictures —as a result of electronic processes which take place in practically empty space. The space occupied at any given moment by electrons is less than the billionth part of the most solid object perceived by our senses, so that the 'material' part of our body could be contained in as little space as occupied by a droplet of water . . ."

In the universe of atomic physics, where old-fashioned tables of the solid type have given place to ones composed of numerous electric charges rushing about with great speed, the miraculous disappearance of matter is no longer miraculous, contends Dr. Booth.

"The physicists assure us that no law of nature would be violated if, for instance, this book should suddenly vanish. Accidentally all the electrons composing it could have moved into a pattern allowing it to fall through the empty spaces composing your hand or desk like the salt running through the top of a salt shaker. The probability of such an event is small, but by no means infinitesimal. It can be defined by a scientifically respectable mathematical formula . . ."

[2] Gotthard Booth, *Religion and Health*, Association Press, New York, 1958.

A cancer might disappear in the same way, he suggests, but as the result of prayer, not accident.

The data of parapsychology throws light on the possible processes in supernormal healing. Experiments in PK, or *psychokinesis* (the direct action of the mind on matter), conducted in the former Parapsychology Laboratory at Duke University and elsewhere, have shown that the mind apparently can influence the fall of dice. These experiments, painstakingly repeated hundreds of times under laboratory controls, make a strong *prima facie* case for the ability of thought to act upon objects without any physical instrumentation.

That this PK force can stimulate growth and healing in plants and animals is indicated by the research of Dr. Bernard Grad at Montreal's McGill University. Biologist Grad has accumulated an impressive body of evidence establishing that, in his own words, "there is a power released by prayer . . . an actual force. . . . Some people can generate this force which is capable of stimulating cell growth in plants and animals."

(Full details of Dr. Grad's controlled experiments, involving prayer for plants and wounded laboratory animals, are contained in my book *The Unexplained*.)

Is it the same force that stimulates plant growth in Dr. Grad's laboratory and regresses tumors in Kathryn Kuhlman's meetings? This seems likely.

What is the attitude of the churches toward spiritual healing?

It is impossible to generalize, of course, but there are signs of at least a new openness.

In 1950, the National Council of Churches—the interdenominational body representing most major Protestant communions in the United States—made a survey to determine how widespread spiritual healing practices were among ministers. The results indicated that more clergymen practice prayer therapy than probably anyone realized.

Of the 460 pastors replying to the questionnaire, 160 had actual cases of healing to report. The techniques employed included prayer alone, the laying on of hands, anointing with holy oil, and various forms of what could be called pastoral counseling.

What kinds of disease were cured?

Some sixty-four were specified, including different forms of cancer (of the lungs, spine, mouth, duodenum, and bone). Most of the respondents said the disease had been diagnosed by a competent physician and in some cases the patients had been given up by doctors.

The survey indicated that Methodist ministers were in the majority among practitioners of spiritual healing, followed by Episcopalians, Lutherans, Baptists, Disciples of Christ, United Brethren, Congregational, Evangelical, and Reformed, in that order.

Healing by prayer and faith, then, is moving out of the theological boondocks of the itinerant revivalist into the Protestant mainstream.

The Roman Catholic Church, of course, always has maintained an awareness of healing by faith and, as we noted in a previous chapter, some of the most astounding cures reported anywhere happen at Lourdes and other shrines.

There are, of course, critics of faith healing, or spiritual healing, in the established churches. But there is evidence that they are not so influential as they once were.

In 1967, the United Church—Canada's largest Protestant communion—issued an official report on faith healing titled *Sickness and Health*. The twenty-page manifesto set forth the views of a committee of theologians, psychologists, and psychiatrists set up to explore the whole question of healing from the standpoint of the Christian faith.

Essentially, the report was a rewrite of one drafted in 1965 by Toronto minister-psychologist Mervyn Dickinson. That first version contained an indiscriminate condemnation of faith healing which—significantly—was watered down in the final draft.

The original 1965 document said: "Faith-healing is not a legitimate ministry of the Church and should be actively discouraged and resisted wherever it is practised."

The revised version said: "Faith healers of the type described above [that is, itinerant revivalists such as Oral Roberts, who was specifically mentioned] do not exercise a legitimate ministry of the Church and should be actively resisted in their practice."

The committee added: "However, while opposing the general run of faith-healers, it would be dangerous to generalize too broadly and presumptuous to pretend ability to judge every case.

"It is well to recognize humbly that there is much in the whole realm of faith-healing which we do not know. Discrimination between the authentic and the spurious is not easy but very important."

These statements are significant because they do recognize that "authentic" faith healing exists, as well as the "spurious."

In his first version, Dr. Dickinson had rejected all faith healing, contending that the very few cures it does achieve "could be effected by a physician or psychotherapist without the dangers which accompany the methods of the faith-healer."

The main criticisms of standard, revival-tent faith healing in the report are:

1. It is based on an inadequate theology which often assumes sickness to be a divine judgment.

2. It has a naïve view of the distinction between "natural" and "supernatural" healing.

3. It works—when it does—usually by suggestion and hysteria and the patient may suffer a relapse that leaves him worse off than he was before.

4. Persons who are not healed may feel that God has rejected them and suffer morbid guilt feelings and spiritual shipwreck.

The United Church document contains a provocative examination of the healing ministry of Christ as described in the New Testament.

The types of illnesses which were cured by Jesus are of interest and importance [the report says].

Leslie D. Weatherhead [former president of the Methodist Church of Great Britian and a noted clergyman-psychologist] has made a notable effort to interpret these illnesses and their cures by correlating the opinions of textual scholars, physicians, and psychologists.

This frequently involves the use of diagnostic terms that are more precise or more acceptable to contemporary thought.

For example, Weatherhead maintains that the term for leprosy covered a variety of skin diseases like psoriasis and eczema.

The woman with hemorrhage who followed Jesus is thought to have been crippled by painful menstruation.

The cripple who waited by Bethesda's pool for 30 years is considered to have been immobilized by neurotic illness.

The translation of first century terms into those of our day is of greatest interest where a psychiatric description is substituted for the attribution of demon possession.

Churchmen with impeccable intellectual and ecclesiastical credentials are supporting the reality of healing through prayer and faith.

". . . Spiritual healing, though rare, is very real," says Dr. Cyril C. Richardson, Washburn Professor of Church History at New York's prestigious Union Theological Seminary, in *Religion and Health*.

"When it comes," he continues, "it can come with a dramatic suddenness and spectacular character which far outdistance modern medicine.

"This is why we must always provide the occasion for it."

Dr. Richardson cites what he calls "marked characteristics" of spiritual cures "which tend to recur in all the accounts." There is often a sudden acute pain. The healing is rapid and permanent. Faith in some form is invariably present. There is an atmosphere of religious expectation. Such cures are infrequent.

Aside from the opinions of scientists and religious men, whose views could come closer together again in our time, possibly due to phenomena such as are cited here, the final decisions as to the validity of inexplicable healings described in this book must rest with my reader. It is he, and he alone, who, after assessing the evidence, will decide about a healing. He is to be the final court of appeal—but only for himself.

Let's now consider in detail six specific Kathryn Kuhlman healings which show characteristics described in this chapter as qualifying as an inexplicable healing.

4

The Case of George Orr

The person who first convinced me that miracles do happen in Kathryn Kuhlman's ministry was George Orr.

This seventy-six-year-old resident of Butler, Pennsylvania, was the second individual to be healed by what Kathryn Kuhlman calls "The Power." That was on May 4, 1947.

During a 1964 Pittsburgh interview Mr. Orr told me about his healing.

In 1925 he was blinded in his right eye, the result of an industrial accident. His injury was concisely described in a document which he gave me to examine, the official report of compensation awarded him by the Pennsylvania Department of Labor and Industry. The case, referred to as Claim Petition No. 27413, was dealt with in a hearing at Butler, Pennsylvania, on March 11, 1927.

The relevant parts of the document were as follows:

> From testimony taken your referee [the state-appointed ajudicator] finds these facts:
>
> That the claimant George G. Orr was injured on December 1, 1925, while at work in the employ of the

Lawrence Foundry Company at Grove City, Pennsylvania.

That while casting molds the claimant suffered an injury to his right eye caused by a splash of molten iron.

That on the date of the injury the claimant visited Dr. C. E. Imbrie, an eye specialist at Butler, Pennsylvania, who found the eye badly burned, which condition resulted in a corneal ulcer.

That as a result of the injury he received, the claimant's vision in his injured eye has been reduced to twenty-one over one hundred . . .

That the eye in its present condition is equivalent to the loss of the use of the member for industrial use.

The report concluded: "the claimant is entitled to compensation . . . for the loss of an eye."

Medical testimony by Dr. Imbrie, the attending ophthalmologist, indicated that the virtually total impairment of vision in the injured eye was permanent.

Actually, in strict fact, the sight of the injured eye was not destroyed. Rather, it was obstructed by a deep corneal scar, the result of the searing of the eyeball by the splash of molten iron. The splinter of metal which did the damage in its molten state was, when it hardened, "the size of a swelled grain of wheat," Orr recalled. The scar it left acted like a blindfold on the eye.

"I could see just the tiniest bit out of the top of the eye by looking over the scar," said Orr. "But for practical purposes the eye was useless."

(The medical data include the fact that injury to the eye was compounded by secondary infection which caused George Orr, as he put it, "six months of solid misery.")

One Sunday in March 1947, Orr and his wife attended a service in Franklin, Pennsylvania, conducted by a young woman named Kathryn Kuhlman. Nothing spectacular happened in that service, apparently, but the Orrs enjoyed it.

Over the next two months they returned several times to hear Kathryn Kuhlman preach.

May 4 was a Sunday. Mr. and Mrs. Orr went to Kathryn Kuhlman's meeting with a young couple they knew. The young man drove.

During the service the evangelist declared flatly that physical healing was just as possible today as spiritual salvation was.

That statement stabbed something awake inside George Orr.

"Right then," he recalled, "I prayed, 'God, please heal my eye.'

"The next moment I felt a tingling in my right eye, as though a mild electric shock were passing through it. Then it began to stream tears. They ran down on to my jacket. I was embarrassed because I couldn't control it."

When the service ended, Orr had trouble negotiating the aisle. He couldn't walk straight.

"I have the strangest feeling," he confided to the young man with him. "Something has come over me that I don't understand."

He says now, "I was under The Power but didn't know it."

On the drive home Orr was aware that something was different. He kept blinking his bad eye which was still running with tears, although they gradually lessened.

Then suddenly he covered his good eye with his hand. In that moment he realized what had happened.

"I can see," he exclaimed. "I can see everything."

And he is still seeing with that eye.

What had taken place?

Well, obviously the corneal scar had melted, or started to melt, during the Kathryn Kuhlman meeting. But what caused this to happen?

Was it a spontaneous recovery? Was the melting of the scar a perfectly natural phenomenon which would have been likely to occur sooner or later?

Not according to the medical opinion that no improvement in the eye could be expected. More than once Orr had asked about the possibility of surgery to restore or at least improve his vision. The reply always was that the corneal scar was too deeply embedded in the underlying structures of the eye to be safely removed. One gathers that it would have been more a case of removing the eye from the scar than vice versa. If the scar went, the eyeball was more than likely to go with it.

The time element in the healing is significant. Why, after twenty years, did the corneal scar melt, when it did, during a faith-healing meeting? True, coincidences do happen but this was a singular one indeed, enough to qualify as at least a sort of miracle of its own.

Moreover, when the Orr case is considered not in isolation but in the context of all the other Kathryn Kuhlman healings, coincidence as a plausible explanation is severely strained. One might almost as well argue that the benefits which follow penicillin treatment are sheer coincidences. Speaking in a technical sense, the only real argument that they're not is a statistical one—that the benefits occur too often to be mere chance. The same argument applies to Kathryn Kuhlman's healings.

Two years after he was healed, George Orr decided to play a joke on Dr. Imbrie, the ophthalmologist who had treated his eye. Confident that he wouldn't be recognized after so long a time, he went to the doctor for an eye examination. In his pocket he carried a copy of the state compensation award which cited Dr. Imbrie's own findings.

After his examination the doctor said that Orr's eyes were in very good condition.

"The right one too?" Orr asked.

"Yes," the doctor replied. "As a matter of fact, it's better than the other one. Why do you mention it?"

With that, Orr handed over the compensation report.

The ophthalmologist read it with obviously mounting astonishment. Then he murmured over and over: "This is something. This is *really* something."

George Orr couldn't have agreed more.

5

The Case of Young Karen

When Karen George was born, on August 3, 1948, her mother remembers, the doctor told Mrs. George after the delivery: "You have a nice, healthy baby girl, with the exception of one thing that's wrong."

"What's that?" Mrs. George asked, feeling a stab of fear, and the doctor said: "She has a club foot."

It was the baby's left foot that was deformed.

"The bottom of the foot was facing up," recalled Mrs. George, when I talked to her in her home in Conway, Pennsylvania, in September 1968, "and in the middle of the bottom of the foot there was a ball of flesh about as big as a walnut. Her toes were scrunched up. And her kneecap wasn't where it should have been—it was twisted around toward the side of her leg." (Karen sat listening on a sofa across the room during our interview.)

The exact cause of club foot is not known. One medical theory is that the fetus assumes a cramped position in the womb and the foot—this sometimes occurs to both feet— is twisted and develops that way.

Cases of club feet vary in seriousness. Mrs. Earl George remembers Karen's as a severe case.

"The doctors involved—and there was more than one—told me a case like hers would take at least twenty years of medical care. And they didn't promise she would be normal even then.

"My husband and I took Karen to the doctor twice a week for the first five months, then about every two weeks. The doctor would tape and bandage the foot, trying to bring it into a more normal position. But after we got the baby home and put her in the crib, the foot would flop back just the way it had been, in spite of the bandages and tape.

"When she was three months old they put this on her."

Mrs. George produced a tiny brace, made of metal and lined with a soft feltlike material. It obviously was designed to fit an infant's foot and leg from the toes to about two inches above the knee.

"When she was six months old, another doctor put this one on her," said Mrs. George, taking another brace—similar to the first but half as large again—out of a dresser drawer.

The evident purpose of the brace was to hold the deformed leg rigid in a more normal position so that over a period of time it would, hopefully, develop correctly.

"When we saw no improvement from the first brace, we changed doctors," said Mrs. George. "Karen was four months old then. We took her to another orthopedist who was recommended to us. He immediately put her in a cast that encased the whole leg and left it on for a month. She cried almost constantly. When they took the cast off, the leg flopped back exactly as it had been before.

"The doctor let her go about a month and then tried another cast. More crying almost day and night. And when he took off that cast, the leg promptly went back into its twisted position.

"The orthopedist said surgery was going to be necessary but the first operation couldn't be done until Karen was two and a half.

"Well, we were very dismayed. We met other parents with children who had the same problem in the doctor's waiting room and they told us of repeated operations, and sometimes after years of treatment the child was still deformed. We knew, too, from talking to other parents and seeing their children that Karen's was a very serious case."

At this point, when the Georges had become aware of the gravity of Karen's deformity and the length of time that might be required for treatment, a woman who came to the door selling soap told them about a young evangelist named Kathryn Kuhlman who had been in Pittsburgh only a year or so. The saleslady said that miraculous healings were taking place every week in Miss Kuhlman's meetings and that maybe God would heal little Karen if they took her to a service.

"We were discouraged enough by the medical treatment's producing no improvement that we decided in desperation to give faith a try, even though it was actually against my religion at the time," Mrs. George recalled with a faint smile. "We belonged to another church then, you see, and I thought seeking divine healing was wrong."

She never forgot her first miracle service.

"I was overwhelmed when Kathryn came out—she looked like an angel. She wore a white dress and she had something that no one else I'd ever seen had. I didn't know at that time that it was the power of the Holy Spirit."

Mrs. George remembers that she wept throughout the service. When Kathryn Kuhlman asked everybody to kneel in prayer and tell the Lord what it was they wanted Him to do for them, Mrs. George knelt and prayed—even though she wasn't used to making requests of God for specific favors. She prayed for Christ to come into her heart, and for Karen's healing.

"I went out of that service in a daze, I was so full of joy," she said. "And the next morning, when I woke up, I felt like a new person. Unknown to me, God had healed me of neuritis. For years I had suffered severe pain, especially in my legs, and on the doctor's advice—he was the one who called it neuritis—wore elastic stockings. Since my healing I haven't worn elastic stockings and there isn't a trace of neuritis in my body."

Her own healing strengthened Mrs. George's faith that Karen could be healed, "even though," she allows, "it was hard to believe that a twisted leg could be straightened, especially after all the medical treatments had accomplished nothing that we could see."

To this day, Kathryn Kuhlman tells the story of Mrs. George arriving at a miracle service, loaded down with Karen and an armful of paraphernalia.

"I looked and there was this woman sitting slap down in front of me with a baby in her arms and three shopping bags full of diapers and baby bottles," says the evangelist with a chuckle.

"Well, I'd been told that sometimes miracle services went on for hours," Mrs. George explained, "and I came prepared for a long session.

"During the healing part of the service Kathryn came down and asked if there was something wrong with the baby. Karen's foot was covered by a blanket so the deformity wasn't visible, but I rolled the blanket back and said she had a club foot.

"Kathryn took the baby in her arms and told the congregation what was wrong with her and asked them all to pray for the healing of the foot. You could see she was deeply touched. It was wonderful. After praying, she gave Karen back to me and said she was going to be all right."

Throughout the rest of the service and all the way home Mrs. George kept peeking at Karen's leg.

"It wasn't perfect but it was straighter than it had been, I was sure of that. And yet was I? I didn't know whether I had enough faith to believe she was going to be healed or not.

"Well, two days later, on Sunday, Mrs. Olsen, our next-door neighbor, came over to see Karen and she suddenly exclaimed, 'Oh, this is wonderful. She's going to be perfectly healed. Look!' And she showed me that the lump on the bottom of Karen's foot had disappeared.

"Now it sounds awfully stupid on my part, I know, but I hadn't noticed the lump was gone, and I don't know just when it happened. But sure enough it was gone.

"My husband Earl and I were overjoyed because the doctor had told us that this lump probably always would remain. He said she was going to have a 'rocking foot,' that's what he called it."

The week after this incident Mrs. George kept an appointment with the orthopedist. After he had examined the child (without making any comment about the disappearance of the lump), Mrs. George told him about taking Karen to Kathryn Kuhlman's meeting.

"He just listened," she recalls, "and then said that if God healed people why did doctors like him have to spend years learning medical skills. He said that Karen needed medical treatment and that she must have it. If money was a problem, 'don't worry about it,' he said, because he would treat her for nothing.

"He told us—my mother-in-law was with me that day—to go and sit in the waiting room and think about it. So I did. I went through a terrible crisis in my mind. In spite of what the doctor had said I knew there was a great change in Karen—that lump was gone—and I wondered why he hadn't admitted it. Suddenly, I made my decision. We put our hats and coats on and left."

Karen George received no further medical treatment for her foot. Her mother took her to Kathryn Kuhlman's miracle services regularly. Over a period of a month the child's foot imperceptibly improved until one day Mrs. George examined it and it was perfectly normal.

"Yes, perfectly normal," she said, "just as it is today. See for yourself."

Karen George, now an attractive young woman of twenty, was sitting on a sofa across from me. She stood up, kicked off her shoes, and walked over to where I was sitting. There was no trace of a limp, I noticed. And her feet were normal—not a lump, not the slightest deformity.

"Her childhood was the same as any other child's," said Mrs. George.

"Yes, I can remember riding tricycles and scooters," added Karen, "you know, doing all the things that the other kids did. I wasn't any different."

Karen's mother mentioned that occasionally they still saw a girl about Karen's age who had had a club foot similar to hers. "What a difference," Mrs. George said. "That girl had operation after operation and she walks with a limp to this day.

"We know that what happened to Karen was a miracle performed by the Lord. We know that Kathryn Kuhlman didn't do it—although she's the Lord's instrument. It was God."

Karen's father confirmed his wife's account.

Now what about documentation?

A sophisticated doctor who had spent considerable time trying to pin down miraculous healings once said to me: "You know, I sometimes wonder if God doesn't want me to find positive proof of a miracle. Everytime I get one that's great, a really outstanding healing that in my own mind I'm certain is a genuine miracle, I'm frustrated when it comes to documentation. The doctor's died, the hospital records have been destroyed or mislaid, an X ray is missing. . . . It's as though God were pulling the rug out from under my feet."

I know that doctor's feeling. In Karen George's case we have a magnificent illustration of what one researcher of difficult subjects called "the law of frustration."

First, what about hospital records? Well, Karen was treated on an out-patient basis and such records, said the Pittsburgh hospital concerned, are kept for only ten years. Since Karen's would be twenty years old, they are unavailable.

Doctors' records? One of the orthopedists who treated the child is dead. The other has declined to release his records of the case.

However, there is tangible evidence which supports the Georges' account—the two braces worn by Karen as an infant. Showing these to an orthopedic surgeon on the staff of a city hospital—a medical specialist who sees and prescribes hundreds of such devices in a year—I asked: "If you found these on the street, knowing nothing about the owner, what could you deduce from examining them?"

Looking at them carefully, the orthopedist replied: "Obviously, of course, they're braces for an infant's leg. It's quite clear from the way they're designed that this was a club foot. As a matter of fact, from this brace I can see quite clearly in my mind what the foot probably looked like."

I asked how long such braces would need to be worn. The reply was quick: "At least until the growing period is over. That means fourteen anyway. Often older."

In summation: We have the testimony of Mr. and Mrs. George that at least two orthopedists called Karen's condition a club foot and said that it would require possibly as long as twenty years' treatment. We have the mother's detailed description of the appearance of the foot—one fully compatible with the reported diagnosis. We have her account of how Karen showed marked improvement after being taken to her first miracle service, the most notable detail being the disappearance of the lump on her foot. We have her testimony that the doctor who examined Karen after this event insisted that she needed further treatment and offered his services without charge if necessary.

Moreover, we have the braces—the kind of thing Thoreau might have been including when he said that circumstantial evidence could be very strong indeed, "as when, for instance, a trout is found in the milk." The braces are perfectly consonant with Mrs. George's description of Karen's deformity.

We have the present evidence of Karen herself: that her feet are normal; and that she was normal throughout childhood, being able to run and jump and ride bikes like any other child her age.

If you could personally examine the braces that Karen George once wore, and then examine her feet as they are today, you would, I submit, find it hard to dispute that something extraordinary happened to this young woman —she and her parents call that something a miracle.

6

The Case of
Dr. E. B. Henry

When Pittsburgh physician E. B. Henry first visited a Kathryn Kuhlman service, he had, by his own confession, "no more faith than a rabbit."

He went, he said, "mainly to please my wife."

That was on November 19, 1950, a date, as it turned out, that Dr. Henry wasn't likely to forget.

He took with him to that miracle service the following afflictions:

1. A painful, chronic sinus condition, located in the right antrum and frontal sinuses, which had been treated medically for more than thirty years.

2. The loss of most of the hearing in his right ear.

3. A broken collarbone which had failed to heal in ten months, the result of a fall downstairs in which he had also injured his right knee.

At first, Dr. Henry had been aware of the fracture to his right clavicle (collarbone) and, indeed, had used his right arm and shoulder more than usual because his knee injury required crutches and then a cane. The knee healed but the collarbone, which had received no treatment, did not knit properly.

An X ray of Dr. Henry's right clavicle, taken on March 28, 1950, indicated a fairly clean fracture near the point midway between the ends. A red, angry-looking lump could be seen on the skin at this spot. Motion of the right arm caused a painful grating sensation, apparently from the movement of the ends of the bones at the break. He diagnosed his own affliction as a "false joint."

After that miracle service, in Franklin, Pennsylvania, Dr. Henry, a graduate of the University of Pittsburgh who practiced medicine until his death in 1963 at the age of 73, wrote a letter to Kathryn Kuhlman telling her what had happened to him. The letter is reproduced in *The Case for Spiritual Healing* by Dr. Don Gross, son-in-law of Dr. Henry. In that letter, dated November 24, 1950, he wrote:

Dear Miss Kuhlman:

This letter is both an expression of gratitude and an apology; gratitude to God and to you (may He bless you always), and an apology to you for not recognizing a healing when it was taking place. I shall try to make this letter as short as possible, so here goes the "blow by blow" account . . .

Saturday, November 18th, was a hard day for me. Up at six A.M., going hard all day until 5:30 P.M., when I arrived home for dinner. Rushed to get ready and drove to Franklin. There in the hotel, I had very little sleep, due to an infected right antrum which caused me no little pain, and an old fracture of the right clavicle which had not healed together but had formed a false joint with a callus around it about the size of a walnut. It had been very painful so that I could put my coat on only with difficulty, and my hand would shake when I endeavored to raise my right arm. I assure you that the pain from my neck down to my wrist was really severe.

Sunday morning: Up again at 6:00 A.M. in order to get breakfast and get out to Faith Temple before 9:00 A.M. I want you to know that I truly had no thought as to any healing for myself. I have always been able to stand pain, so my chief concern was for my wife, who had her left breast removed in April for signet-cell carcinoma (a very malignant type), and my fear that she might have metastases. . . .

During your healing period you began to state that there was a "a sinus opening up. Someone is regaining hearing in an ear" (I have been deaf in my right ear for at least 15 years). You went on to say, "I see a lump the size of a walnut beginning to dissolve." My dear wife nudged me and whispered, "She means you," but I, just thinking of her, felt nothing but a burning in my right ear which I thought was the result of mental suggestion.

Then you said, "This is a man. I do not want you to lose this healing. Please speak up." I can see you now as you looked earnestly in our direction waving your left hand almost directly at our group and at the same time pounding the pulpit with your right fist. My wife kept nudging me but even when you said that the man had a burning in his ear, I couldn't believe that I was being healed. After all, I had asked nothing for myself. I was accustomed to the deafness in my right ear and gave it no thought.

I drove the eighty-five miles home through the rain, a condition not conducive to helping sinusitis. On the way home my wife kept speaking to me in an ordinary tone of voice. She was sitting beside me *on my right*. Then she called my attention to my ability to hear her and we both realized I was not asking her to repeat. Just after we arrived home, all of a sudden I had to blow my nose. My sinus had opened and the pain had gone. The antrum kept draining freely all evening. I slept well all night and in the morning I was entirely free of drainage and pain.

To add to my amazement, I found that I was able to use my right arm in normal motion without pain. I cannot state that the hearing in my right ear is perfect but I need not turn my left ear to my wife and ask her to repeat. Perhaps the rest of my hearing will return gradually . . .[1]

Dr. Henry's symptoms of pain in his arm and limitation of motion disappeared in one day. An X ray taken for another purpose on June 20, 1952, showed a perfectly knit bone, and an examination of the skin of the chest showed no difference between the right and left sides. The walnut-size lump had vanished. The healing of the fracture was complete and perfect for the thirteen years Dr. Henry lived after his healing.

In the Spring 1955 issue of *Tomorrow* magazine, Dr. Don Gross, a psychologist and Episcopal priest, reported on his father-in-law's healing. This prompted an inquiry from a California surgeon who asked to examine copies of the X rays taken after the healing of Dr. Henry's collarbone. Subsequently this surgeon wrote Dr. Gross about his impressions, which are quoted in *The Case for Spiritual Healing*.

On X ray One you can see distinctly the proximal part of the clavicula and the line of fracture [the surgeon said in his letter]. The distal end of the bone is not visible probably due to a strong atrophy of the peripheral bone distal from the fracture.

On the basis of this X ray, however, one is not entitled to make the diagnosis of a "false joint." I also feel that your definition of a "false joint" is misleading. You write "such a condition means that the fracture does not knit." This is correct. But it is incorrect to continue, "The outer covering

[1] Don Gross, *The Case for Spiritual Healing*, Thomas Nelson & Sons, New York, 1958.

of the bone grows over each broken end and a callus grows around the fractured area."

Now, that is the description of a normal bone healing but surely not of a "false joint." A "false joint" is always characterized by the lack of new bone formation and you will never find in those cases a "painful lump" as was the case with Dr. Henry.

On the X ray and clinical basis I actually have the impression that the fracture healed without any "false joint" in a completely normal way, and that the remnant was a periostal thickening as shown in the second X ray more than two years after the fracture occurred.

I do not deny psychic influences in the suddenly improved pains and movements in this case but I am unable to declare it as a healing of a collar bone "false joint" due to prayer.

Dr. Henry himself made a detailed reply to the surgeon's comments, noting among other things that the surgeon had examined only less-than-clear reproductions of the X rays of his collarbone and not the originals.

I have read with interest the letter you received from Dr. L. [he wrote to his son-in-law, Dr. Gross]. I feel that he is rather too cynical in regard to the healings which took place in connection with the fracture of my right clavicle. Let us review the case.

On January 7, 1950, due to a fall, the right patella was struck with such a downward force that all the tendinous and ligamental attachments to the upper and lateral aspects of the patella were completely torn loose and the patella was located down over the head of the tibia.

In addition to that, the anterior half of the knee capsule was split wide open exposing the cartilages of the knee. It was necessary to put a hollow silver pin laterally through the patella and wire the ligaments and tendons back in position. Of course it was necessary to close the knee capsule.

I was informed by the orthopedic surgeon that "a man your age, 63 years, cannot expect to get off without some stiffness of your knee."

I was up and around on crutches in less than a week and by the middle of February the cast was removed and I was given an elastic bandage. I then started using a cane and in another week the surgeon said to take the elastic bandage off and "use that knee." I did just that, in spite of the pain, and to this day I have absolutely no limitation of motion. By the end of June I was walking around without a cane.

Now, does it sound reasonable that my knee should heal so well and a simple fracture of the clavicle should take ten months? I am sorry Dr. L. cannot see the original X rays but I must take issue with him when he states that "a false joint is always characterized by lack of bone formation and *never* by a painful lump." He should know that circumstances alter cases. I kept using crutches and cane and thus prevented union of the bone. That nature tried to heal is evidenced by the fibrous callus formation. The fact that the proximal end of the bone was seen is evidence that the fractured ends had been misplaced by use of cane and crutches. Then also false motion could be felt. The callus was much larger than would have been the case in a completely normal healing and it was an angry red and extremely tender and painful after ten months.

As to psychic influence, that is completely out. My entire religious and scientific training had taught me that the age of miracles was past and I walked out of that meeting with no thought that any "healing" had taken place.

Afterward, when I realized that I was able to hear with my right ear and when my sinuses drained freely that night and I was able to use my right arm without pain, then I remembered how Miss Kuhlman had said, "This man is receiving a healing of sinus trouble, his right ear is regaining its hearing, and there is a lump, the size of a walnut, beginning to dissolve." That was in November

1950 and, though I had suffered from frontal sinusitis and antrum trouble every year since I was a freshman in high school, 1908, I have had none since. Personally, I am convinced that nothing is impossible with God . . .

The Laymen's Movement for a Christian World, an inter-denominational group which sponsors seminars on prayer therapy at Wainright House, Rye, New York, set up a Commission for the Study of Spiritual Healing in the 1950s. With New York psychiatrist Dr. Robert W. Laidlaw as chairman, the Commission was comprised of a number of experts in medical and other pertinent scientific disciplines who examined and evaluated cases of purported supernormal healing brought to their attention. They rejected many cases on such grounds as insufficient documentation, misdiagnosis, the possibility of natural remission or delayed response to medical treatment, relapse, and so on.

The Commission studied Dr. Henry's case, including an examination of the before-and-after X rays of his right clavicle. On May 10, 1957, a majority opinion was reached that the case was acceptable to the Commission as having sufficient verification to establish it as an authentic healing by spiritual means.

7

The Case of
Mrs. Virgil Litten

"A new heart will I give you," the Bible says in Ezekiel 36:26. And for Mrs. Virgil Litten these words have become literal truth. And not via a transplant.

In April 1959, when she was forty-eight, Mila Litten was found to be suffering from what her doctor called "very, very serious heart disease." In fact, "a bout of pneumonia would have killed her—with her heart, she'd never have made it."

Mrs. Litten and her physician, Dr. James Blackann, an osteopath, told me about her healing in an interview in September 1968. We talked over coffee in the spacious living room of the doctor's home in Youngstown, Ohio.

(It is pertinent to clarify the professional and legal status of a D.O.—Doctor of Osteopathy—in the United States. An osteopath combines standard medical treatments—drug therapy and surgery—with bone manipulation "to normalize body structure." In Ohio, as in most of our other states, D.O.'s write the same certification examinations as M.D.'s and have exactly the same rights and privileges under the law. In California, the D.O.'s and M.D.'s have officially amalgamated. One indication of the esteem in which some osteopaths are held is that they have been chosen as personal physicians by a number of prominent people today, including New York's Governor Nelson Rockefeller.)

Dr. Blackann had admitted Mrs. Litten to the hospital in 1959 for a comprehensive cardiac evaluation.

"In my examination," he said, "I had detected a skip beat—an irregular beat—of the heart, and also swelling of the feet and ankles.

"The hospital tests, which included an electroencephalogram and cardiac X rays, confirmed my suspicions. Mrs. Litten had a gross enlargement of the left ventricle, indicating that the valve between the left auricle and the left ventricle of the heart was very badly dilated and leaking. The condition is called mitral stenosis."

Dr. Blackann attributed the valve damage to a bout of rheumatic fever Mrs. Litten had had when she was thirty-two. He felt that open heart surgery to repair the deformed valve was indicated, but the cardiologists consulted on the case suggested postponing the operation until less radical treatment could be tried. Mrs. Litten was put on a strict regimen of medication, diet, and bed rest. She showed enough improvement over a period of several months for the heart surgery to be temporarily shelved. However, her heart remained abnormal and her activities were restricted.

Dr. Blackann later sent Mrs. Litten into the hospital for further cardiac evaluations at regular intervals. These indicated that her heart was slowly deteriorating and once again valve surgery was contemplated.

A cardiac evaluation made at the Youngstown Osteopathic Hospital in May 1966 confirmed the original diagnosis: "Rheumatic heart disease with mitral stenosis and auricular fibrillation [irregular heartbeat]."

Cardiac X rays at that time showed "evidence of mitral valvular disease with a considerable degree of left atrial enlargement and right ventricular enlargement. This appearance is consistent with mitral stenosis. The degree of left atrial enlargement is considerably more marked than on the most recent previous study dated July 28, 1965."

The cardiologist summed up with an overall assessment and a recommendation: "There is definite evidence of further left auricular enlargement since the last examination . . . and further evidence of increasing pulmonary hypertension. For this reason I think . . . the time is nearing for the need of a mitral commissurotomy."

(A mitral commissurotomy is surgery to correct the constricted heart valve.)

How did the heart condition affect Mrs. Litten? How did she feel?

"Terrible, at first," she said. "I couldn't do anything. I was short of breath, my ankles and feet would swell, I got pain in my heart if I just overexerted myself talking.

"There was a point when I felt certain I was going to die and I realized I was afraid to die."

Mrs. Litten said she lost her fear of death when she discovered Kathryn Kuhlman.

"We had heard her on the radio for some time," Mrs. Litten recalled, "and my husband and I started going to her services. It was there that we gave our hearts to Christ, and oh, what a difference that made."

That was in 1961. With her new faith Mrs. Litten's spirits improved, and her health. She had more energy and was able to resume a more normal life. But she knew she wasn't healed. The ominous heaviness in her chest returned whenever she tried to do anything too strenuous, and the swelling of her feet and ankles reminded her that what she needed was nothing less than a new heart.

After the cardiac evaluation in May 1966, facing the prospect once again of the radical operation she had dreaded and avoided for so long, Mila Litten began praying in earnest that God would heal her.

In October 1966, she underwent heart surgery of a different sort—among a crowd of three thousand people in a Kathryn Kuhlman miracle service.

"Of course, I'll never forget it," she said, beginning to weep. "How could I?

"It was at a miracle service in Pittsburgh. Virgil [her husband] was ushering and I was sitting with friends. I had gone many times asking the Lord to heal me and it hadn't happened. Suddenly, as I was standing singing a hymn, I thought to myself, 'You are standing in God's way!'

"I can't explain it but I just knew that somehow my trying so hard to be healed was actually blocking God from healing me. It just seemed as if, at that moment, something in me said, 'Well, Mila, why don't you get out of the way?'

"So I said, 'Dear Lord, get me out of the way.' The next instant I went down under The Power!

"Everything began to whirl around me. I swayed and fell back into my seat. I didn't pass out. But my head was throbbing like a hammer and my heart was pounding inside my chest as if it were going to leap out of it. I'd never experienced anything like it before.

"Then, the weight lifted from my chest and I felt a great sense of lightness, of floating. I could breathe! I could take deep breaths! . . . And then I knew I had been healed."

Kathryn Kuhlman was aware of the healing at the time

and told Mrs. Litten: "God's just given you a new heart. You're going out of here a different woman than when you came in."

From that moment, Mrs. Litten felt buoyant, vital, reborn. She lost years in appearance (she now looks ten years younger than in a photograph taken ten years ago). Her eyes, which had been dull, recaptured their twinkle. She had more energy than she'd had since childhood.

But she couldn't help wondering: What will the doctor say? Will he admit it's a miracle?

"Frankly, I was astounded," said Dr. Blackann when I asked him how he had felt about his patient's improvement. He fingered his beard and chuckled softly.

Mrs. Litten came in to see me and I listened to her heart. And then I listened again. And then I looked at her chart, and listened again. I couldn't believe it. Her clinical symptoms had subsided. The cardiac murmur was gone. Her heart seemed perfectly normal. In my experience as a doctor I'd never seen a similar dramatic change in this kind of heart condition.

So I said, "Mila, what have you been doing? What's happened?" And she smiled and said, "Why? Do you notice a difference?" And I said, "Well, frankly, yes I do." Then she told me she had had a heart healing at Kathryn Kuhlman's meeting.

My reply was pretty abrupt. "Come on, I said, are you trying to be funny?" And she said, "What do you mean? Don't you believe in divine healing?"

And I said, "Yes I believe in divine healing. But I don't believe in Kathryn Kuhlman healing. Kathryn Kuhlman never healed anybody of anything."

Then Mrs. Litten explained. "Don't misunderstand me," she said. "I was at Kathryn Kuhlman's meeting and received a healing from God."

Well, I was intrigued. I sent her into the hospital for tests. The cardiac X ray showed a definite decrease in the size of the heart.

Medically, I would say that this kind of change could have occurred if she had had the open heart surgery—and even then it would have been quite dramatic—but without the surgery? No, you would *never* expect it. To me this was miraculous.

Normally this kind of heart disease progressively worsens without surgery. You just don't get spontaneous remissions. You see, Mila Litten's whole heart has changed. It's as if it had been rebuilt.

"Clinically," said Dr. Blackann, "Mrs. Litten's condition continues to be excellent.

"She has a blood pressure of 112 over 68 to 70 and this doesn't vary. She stays very, very normal. In fact, Dr. Paul Dudley White, this country's leading cardiologist, said a person who is sixty years old and has a blood pressure of 110 over 70 is to be congratulated."

And what did Mila Litten say?

She chuckled: "From being a semi-invalid, now I just go, go, go . . ."

8

The Case of Dr. Bennett Hill

For Alice Hill, October 20, 1967, is a day etched in painful memory. That was when her husband Ben, a physician, descended into the valley of the shadow of death as far as it is possible for a person to go and return. In fact, medically speaking, he went past the point of no return—and that's why he's in this book.

Bennett Hill is a pediatrician in Youngstown, Ohio. Educated at St. Joseph's College in Overbrook, Pennsylvania, and the Philadelphia College of Osteopathy, he was in general practice as an osteopathic physician for seventeen years before taking his residency in pediatrics at Cleveland's Brentwood Hospital.

Dr. Hill and his wife described their ordeal to me in great detail during an interview in their Youngstown home in September 1968.

Mrs. Hill remembered that about a week before Dr. Hill's brush with death, he complained about brief spells of double vision and numbness in his right thumb.

"He went to an internist," said Alice Hill, "who couldn't find anything physically wrong and put the symptoms down

97

to tension and anxiety from Ben's starting practice as a pediatrician. However, to be on the safe side, he wanted him to have a brain scan and an EEG—electroencephalogram—but Ben couldn't, he said, because he was preparing to go to San Francisco to write his first certifying exams in pediatrics. The tests were put off until he got back."

But tragedy struck before he left for San Francisco.

"It was a Friday," Alice Hill recalled. "Ben had gotten in late the night before from a house call so I'd let him sleep late. A phone call for him came from the hospital about 11:00 A.M. and I went to wake him up. He said he felt sick, that his vision was double and his ear seemed plugged. I called an internist and made a five o'clock appointment for him, but by the time I got back to the bedroom he was much worse.

"Really worried, now, I called the doctor he shared an office with and said I wanted him to take a look at Ben and I would drive him right over. By the time we got to the office Ben had taken a grand mal seizure and they rushed him to emergency at the hospital.

"His condition was obviously grave but they couldn't be sure of the diagnosis. An electrocardiogram and a cardiac arteriogram were normal, showing it wasn't his heart. They suspected then that it was an embolism—a blood clot plugging an artery—but they didn't know where or what had caused it.

"They did a tracheotomy—an incision into the windpipe—as he was having great difficulty breathing. By this time, Ben was totally paralyzed except for his eyes, which he could move up and down but not laterally."

The final diagnosis was: occlusion of the basilar artery, the main blood vessel to the brain. The prognosis?

"Well, let's put it this way," one doctor who was in-

volved with the case told me, "every day we walked in we
expected him to be dead. There were, at that time, five
similar cases in the medical literature that we could find
and they all died within two months. Even if he did live, we
expected massive brain damage and a progressive deteri-
oration to the state of a vegetable."

Alice Hill recalled: "One of the neurologists on the case
told me that Ben was already past what textbook knowledge they had about such a condition and that most of
their information about it came from postmortems."

What about Dr. Hill himself? I asked him if he, during
those first hours when he realized that his mind was
trapped within a totally paralyzed body, had made a diagnosis of his own case.

"Yes," he replied evenly. "My diagnosis was massive
occlusion of the basilar artery."

And his prognosis?

"Terminal." But he smiled. "However, I didn't believe
for a moment, in spite of my own medical prognosis, that
I was going to die. I knew I would recover."

For nearly a month Dr. Hill lay in the intensive care
unit of the hospital, wrapped in paralysis, communicating
with his wife by means of a code they had worked out
based on the number of times he blinked his eyes.

The attending doctors—there was a team of them;
several were personal friends of the patient—did little because there was nothing they could do. Their unanimous
medical opinion was that he was already more dead than
alive.

But one doctor, a friend of Ben Hill's, didn't agree.
Acquainted with Kathryn Kuhlman's healing ministry, this
doctor asked the evangelist if she would visit Dr. Hill and
pray for him. She agreed, if the request came from a member of the Hill family. Alice Hill readily assented.

Before Kathryn Kuhlman made her visit, the doctor whose idea it was discussed faith healing with one of the neurologists on the case.

"I asked him bluntly, 'What do you think of Ben's chances?' He said, 'I don't even want to talk about it.' But I persisted: 'Do you really think he's going to die?' He said, 'Yes.' I said, 'Would you call it a miracle if he survived?' He said, 'Yes, I would.' He had no objection to Kathryn Kuhlman praying, he added, 'but it wouldn't do any good.' "

Kathryn Kuhlman came to Mr. Hill's hospital room on a Sunday afternoon, almost a month after he took ill. Alice Hill remembers the experience vividly.

"My feelings when I met her are very hard to put into words. This woman is just so, so—well, she has such strength and such warmth and such magnetism and such obvious love for people and such a spiritual quality about her. I've never seen anybody like her.

"She's Christ-like, that's the only adequate way I can put it. She took my hand and gripped Ben's shoulder and we knew she really cared. She cried and I cried and Ben was crying inside too. She brought this great sense of peace into the room. And when she prayed for Ben, and said she was absolutely sure he was going to be all right, I couldn't doubt it. We felt that we were in the right hands —God's hands."

Although he couldn't tell anybody at the time, Ben Hill had a remarkable experience when Kathryn Kuhlman laid hands on him and prayed for his healing. He describes a sensation like "pins and needles shooting up and down his legs." He also had a deep inner sense that all was well.

Within the next two days he got his first bodily movement besides the eye-blinks; he was able to wiggle a thumb and a finger. From then on, movement gradually returned to him like a slow but relentless tide advancing over his body.

As a result of meeting Kathryn Kuhlman, Bennett and Alice Hill underwent a profound religious experience, one which straightened out their "scrambled thinking" about just what they, as halfhearted Protestants, really did believe and, more important, what their purpose in life was going to be from now on.

They decided that when Ben regained his full strength they would "start a clinic of some kind where Kathryn could send families with children who needed help and couldn't afford it, and this would be our contribution to her work." It was after she had written Kathryn Kuhlman about this decision that Alice was healed herself and got a taste of what it's like to "go under The Power."

"Ben and I went to a miracle service in Pittsburgh," she recalled. "He was in a wheelchair. My problem was my feet. They just generally hurt. I had been supposed to go in for vein surgery but never got around to it. Also, I was a mild diabetic but I had put off starting medication for that.

"We went to that service not expecting Ben to get up out of the wheelchair and walk—although we didn't think it was impossible—but more in hope of finding the spiritual peace we longed for. I was depressed and upset about a lot of things.

"Well, nothing happened during the service—to us, that is. Oh, we watched the people get healed and fall flat when Kathryn laid hands on them, but when you don't know their actual condition you don't know whether they were really healed or not, and whether the collapsing was merely emotion.

"Well, after the service I did feel faintly disappointed—not in Kathryn but for Ben or myself. I didn't know quite what to think. Then we met Kathryn going to her car. She came up and cupped my face in her hands and I went—well, a friend grabbed me, otherwise I would have hit the sidewalk. To tell you the absolute truth, I have never experienced anything like it in my life. I've fainted twice in my life, and it wasn't that feeling of losing consciousness. In fact, I was very conscious, as though everything that was happening was indelibly etched in my brain. But I couldn't see anyone or anything but Kathryn. I closed my eyes but I could still see her and it was as though there wasn't anybody else in the whole world. I was there and I wasn't there at the same time. In a moment, everything seemed swimming in light instead of gloom. Kathryn seemed very beautiful and illuminated.

"I have never had a spiritual experience like it. It was electrifying, like being turned on with spiritual LSD.

"Later, I realized that my feet—which should have been ready to fall off after standing throughout that miracle service—didn't hurt at all. And they haven't hurt since."

Today, Dr. Bennett Hill has taken his certifying examinations in pediatrics (he said he failed to answer only five out of the five hundred questions) and is doing consultations on a part-time basis. He is not yet completely normal. His speech is thick and he walks with the aid of two canes. But his progress is steady and he expects to see the complete fulfillment of Kathryn Kuhlman's words, spoken when he had been surrendered to death by his medical colleagues: "He is going to be all right."

Dr. Hill describes his recovery as "like coming back from the dead, a resurrection."

In Kathryn Kuhlman's ministry there have been a number of healings of normally terminal conditions, some instantaneous or very rapid, and others, like Bennett Hill's, slow and gradual. Why the difference is a mystery which even the evangelist herself doesn't attempt to answer. But she is certain of one thing: In every healing—whether it takes a second, a minute, a day, a week, a month, a year— it is the same power that does the work.

A neurologist on the staff of a major metropolitan hospital listened with great interest to my account of the case of Bennett Hill. When I had finished I asked him: "What do you think of it? Or let me put it this way, if Ben Hill had been your patient, what would your prognosis have been?"

He stroked his chin and smiled faintly. Then he said: "I'll answer by telling you something that happened very recently. A group of researchers have been polling neurologists all over the country about various conditions and one of the questions was whether we had ever seen a case of occlusion of the basilar artery that recovered. I can only say that I doubt very much if they expect to get any affirmative answers to that question."

9

The Case of a
Four-Year-Old Boy

In this case, an added strength is that not one but two medical specialists diagnosed the ailment and then attested to the healing. However, the law of frustration raises its enigmatic head again. The case is an anomalous one inasmuch as the healing, though genuinely inexplicable, was oddly imperfect.

On August 29, 1953, a four-and-a-half-year-old boy was brought to Dr. Clair King of Canton, Ohio, for treatment of an eye injury. Dr. King and his son, William, with whom he has a joint practice, are opthalmologists; that is, they specialize in diseases of the eye. Dr. King was able to reconstruct the case exactly from his records. He described the details to me in an interview at his office in September 1968. The gray-haired physician spoke in very specific terms.

"The boy had been hit in the eye by a piece of flying glass," said Dr. King. "He had—and I'm reading here from the case card—a large through-and-through laceration of the cornea with a prolapse of the iris."

The cornea, sometimes described as the window of the

eye, is what lets the light in and makes vision possible at all. The iris is the pulpy colored part of the eye—made up of tissue and blood vessels—which lies behind the cornea. In this case, the cornea was torn wide open and the iris was protruding through the wound.

There was a drawing of the boy's eye on the case card— made by Dr. King at the time of his initial examination— showing the lesion as a very large one, extending most of the way across the cornea.

It was serious [Dr. King said]. We operated right away to repair the damage. The procedure was to cut off the protruding part of the iris—we call it excision of the pro- lapsed iris—and pull a flap of conjunctiva—the thin, glass- like membrane that covers the white of the eye and the inside of the lids—over the wound for it to heal.

The next record is on the 30th, the next day. It showed that the flap was holding and there was only slight inflam- matory reaction. In other words, the eye was healing fairly well.

However, on September 8—that is, a little over a week later—there was trouble. The eye was white, which was good, but there was a protrusion of the iris. The original laceration had split open because of pressure inside the eye and the iris was projecting through it again.

On the 12th, another examination revealed that the eye looked good except for the prolapse of the iris. We de- cided to operate again on the 15th to repeat the procedure of excising the prolapsed iris and repairing the wound.

Well, the boy was admitted to the hospital on the 14th. When we—my son and I—saw him the next day in the operating room, the wound had healed. My notation on my record is "No operation necessary."

Dr. King and his son were surprised and puzzled. In the three days since the boy's eye had last been examined the protruding iris had, of its own accord apparently, receded into its proper position and the corneal lesion had neatly healed, leaving only a small scar.

"We sent the boy home," Dr. King said, "and the eye, on later examination, proved to be well healed.

"We thought that what had happened was peculiar— very peculiar—but we shrugged and filed the case card away in our records. At that time I knew nothing about spiritual healing. It wasn't until later that I discovered what had happened to the boy between the time we examined him on the 12th and our seeing him again in the operating room on the 15th."

What had happened?

Dr. King chuckled. "His mother had taken him to a Kathryn Kuhlman miracle service in Youngstown and had asked prayer for him for healing. Later, I joked with Kathryn about it and said, 'You cheated us out of an operation.' "

(Had the second operation taken place, the boy's vision would still have been impaired; his sight was beyond medical help and the surgery would only have repaired the open wound. The boy didn't suffer, then, by not having the second operation.)

I asked Dr. King—who took his postgraduate training in ophthalmology at the University of Pennsylvania and his residency at Brooklyn's Kings County Hospital—if such an eye injury, medically speaking, could heal spontaneously.

"Well, I've never seen it happen," he said, "and I've seen hundreds of such lesions of the eye. They don't heal themselves. Let's put it this way: I just don't think it's possible.

"You see, in this case the iris was sticking out through the wound and as long as that iris was in there, the wound wouldn't heal. It would be like sticking a piece of cloth into a wound; the edges of tissue wouldn't come together and you couldn't get it to heal.

"Now, if there were no prolapse of the iris a corneal laceration could heal by itself, but it would take longer than this one did.

"But I have never seen another case where a prolapsed iris went back into place and the perforation of the cornea healed."

What was the normal prognosis in such a case without surgery?

"Three things could happen," Dr. King said.

"First, there would be a continually open wound.

"Second, the patient probably would develop an infection from the open wound and eventually it would destroy the eye and the entire eyeball would have to be removed.

"Or, three, if the eye continually drained through the open wound it would become what we call a soft eye, and that is an unhealthy eye that gradually degenerates."

The last notation on the boy's case card, dated January 9, 1954, read: "Good cosmetic result, the eye quiet [i.e., free of inflammation]."

There are several unusual features to this case, then, on the evidence of the medical record and the testimony of the attending physician. To recapitulate:

1. Within three days—from Saturday, when the doctor examined him, to Tuesday, when he was seen in the operating room—the boy's prolapsed iris returned to its proper position of its own accord, something which the attending opthalmologist says he has never seen in other cases and which he regards as "not possible."

2. The large, through-and-through laceration of the cornea, which had split open after surgery, spontaneously healed during the same three-day period, so that no further treatment of the eye was necessary.

3. The expected outcome in such a case, without surgery—in contradistinction to what actually happened—would be infection or degeneration of the eye resulting in its destruction.

Moreover, the two doctors attesting to the case had no interest in spiritual healing at the time and therefore cannot plausibly be accused of letting their religious convictions color their clinical observations or cloud their medical judgment.

However, a crucial question remains: What about the boy's sight?

In the injured eye he retained only 20–200 vision, or about 10 percent. This sight loss was caused not by the corneal lesion as such but by the rupture of the crystalline lens capsule which allowed fluid to drain into the lens, clouding it and producing what is called a corneal cataract. The window of the eye, in other words, was frosted over and vision correspondingly reduced.

This anomalous healing—the inexplicable recession of the prolapsed iris and the abnormally rapid closing of the corneal wound, yet without restoration of normal vision in the eye—raises many riddles. None of them, however, lies within the bounds of medicine. They are theological riddles: Why was one aspect of the disease cured but not the other? Was it due to a limitation of the healing power? Or did God (since we are speaking theologically) have a reason of His own for the partial healing? If so, is the reason inscrutable or can we at least guess at it? And can an imperfect, albeit inexplicable healing, be considered a "miracle"?

This case is significant because it reflects one aspect of the Kathryn Kuhlman ministry—the fact that not all the healings are perfect, complete. Similar anomalies crop up frequently. A woman is healed of diabetes, say, while a coexisting spinal disease remains. Or a man regains his sight but retains his deafness. Or, again, a person's arthritis is greatly relieved but not totally cured.

It is only proper that theological questions should be addressed to a theologian. Dr. Don Gross, the Pittsburgh Episcopal priest and psychologist mentioned earlier, has brooded long and hard on the enigma of spiritual healing. I asked him about this matter of "anomalous" healings.

"Perhaps they shouldn't be considered anomalies," Dr. Gross said. "Maybe they should be considered the way things usually are, in the sense that all healing is by its nature imperfect or incomplete. Nobody, after all, returns to the optimum physical condition he was in at, say, age twenty-one.

"The logical result of absolutely perfect healing would be physical immortality. All healing is temporary in the sense that it merely postpones but does not indefinitely defer physical death.

"Theologically, spiritual healings are eschatological in nature—that is, ultimate realities are shown to us in glimpses, in breakthroughs, which await their full realization at the day of the final triumph of God.

"A spiritual healing is a promise, if you like. After all, even Lazarus, who was raised from the dead by Christ, in St. John's Gospel, is not running around the Holy Land today. One day he died again. His physical resurrection— his healing—was only temporary.

"A spiritual healing is by its nature imperfect, even the most dramatic one. It symbolizes the battle between the power of God and the chaotic disorder of creation out of which God is trying to bring order and meaning and beauty and perfection.

"It's the old story of life versus death, wholeness versus disintegration, light versus darkness. And although the movement is toward the ultimate triumph of God, nevertheless that triumph is not complete here and now. So spiritual healings, which are but a sign or promise of that ultimate triumph, are not absolutely perfect, complete, and permanent."

In this view, the healings in Kathryn Kuhlman's ministry, whether they are relatively complete or incomplete, have one essential meaning: Hope. They point to a reality deeper than the chaos, darkness, and disintegration we are so often confronted by.

The little boy's case at least implies to all of us: You are not alone.

10
Instant Diagnosis

On a Sunday in May 1968, Dr. James Blackann was standing at the back of Youngstown's crowded Stambaugh Auditorium during a regular Kathryn Kuhlman service. Suddenly he heard the evangelist say: "Somebody at the back of the auditorium is having a leg healing."

"I was surprised," said osteopath Blackann, "because this was a regular worship service and not a meeting specifically for healing.

"Miss Kuhlman repeated, 'This is a leg healing. Someone who's had varicose veins or some similar condition of the leg. . . . You're not expecting healing but you got it anyway.'

"Well, this was the strangest thing to me. I had chronic phlebitis—inflammation of a vein with breakdown of tissue —in the left leg. But I said, 'No, that couldn't be me.'

"Then Miss Kuhlman repeated, 'It's someone at the back.' And I thought again, 'But it couldn't be me. Why, I didn't even ask for help.' Immediately Miss Kuhlman said, 'No, you didn't ask for help but you've been healed anyway.

Take it, and let me know.' Then she went on with the service."

Later, on his way home, Dr. Blackann said he realized that all pain and swelling—of which he had had a considerable amount—had left his leg. The phlebitis did not return.

"And I had a bad case," he said. "My car door had slammed on my leg about two years before. I had pain and swelling—lots of it. The extreme medical procedure in a case like this is to go in surgically and debride—that is, remove—the affected tissues and muscle. That would leave a big hole in your leg which, of course, would heal.

"Well, I was in the hospital for a while. I didn't have the surgery because we were able to get the blood supply back to the affected area. However, it left nothing but pain, very severe pain. That's gone completely since my healing."

Dr. Blackann said he had never mentioned his leg condition to Kathryn Kuhlman, nor was it conceivable that anyone else had since only he and his wife knew about it.

This strange phenomenon—instant *diagnosis* of a condition in the audience and a knowledge of where and when the healing power is at work—is a consistent feature of the Kuhlman ministry. Ask the evangelist, as I have, how she does it, and she invariably replies: "The Spirit tells me . . ."

She admits to being as baffled as anybody else by this.

"People ask me what I have that others don't," she said to me once over coffee in her Pittsburgh office. "Well, to be perfectly honest I don't know what I have. And I don't think much about it.

"I can only say that many times my mind is so surrendered to the Spirit that I know the exact body being healed: the sickness, the affliction, and in some instances, the very sin in their lives. And yet I could not pretend to tell you *why* or *how!*

"There have been times when I have felt faith so permeate every part of my being that I have dared to say and do things which, had I trusted to my own understanding or reason, I would never have done. Yet it flowed through every word and act with such irresistible power that I literally stood in wonder at the mighty works of the Lord."

Let's give the skeptics their innings. Maybe Kathryn Kuhlman's workers, who are circulating through the congregation during the meetings, tip her off about individuals and their ailments. Or, is she just a lucky guesser? After all, in a crowd of several thousand people at a faith-healing meeting you're bound to have represented just about any ailment you want to mention. Other skeptics might go so far as to suggest that the persons the evangelist picks out are "plants"—confederates who've been put up to it.

My investigation has convinced me that none of these explanations stands up. In fact, knowing Kathryn Kuhlman and her ministry as I do, it is for me ludicrous and distasteful even to mention them. However, I realize that the honest skeptic has a perfect right to question everything. So let's consider the possibility of a normal explanation for Kathryn Kuhlman's diagnostic powers.

In the first place, most of the persons she picks out for diagnosis are unknown to her. Or, if they are known to her (which is in rare cases) she usually knows nothing about their having the affliction she describes. In Dr. Blackann's case, he was not unknown to the evangelist. But by his testimony she knew nothing about his phlebitis. Even if she had heard or surmised that he was ill, it could have been anything from sinus trouble to fallen arches.

Is it possible that she saw Dr. Blackann limping or favoring his left leg? Well, this is a possibility but it seems to me an incredibly farfetched one. Ah yes, the skeptic might retort, but not as farfetched as what you're asking us to believe. My reply would be that that depends on the evidence.

In many instances, the people whose diseases are diagnosed are attending their very first miracle service. And often their ailments are such that they have no visible symptoms.

Consider the case of Dr. E. B. Henry mentioned earlier. He had, you remember, chronic sinusitis, deafness in his right ear, and a painful lump the size of a walnut on his collarbone. At his first miracle service he heard the evangelist say, as she looked in his direction: "Someone's sinus is opening up. Someone is regaining hearing in an ear. And I see a lump the size of a walnut beginning to dissolve."

Dr. Henry said that despite his wife's elbow in his ribs he did not acknowledge that he was the person being spoken about. And he left the service without telling the evangelist.

This happens not infrequently. People whose afflictions have been diagnosed and healed go away without mentioning them to the evangelist. Often they don't realize they have been healed—as Dr. Henry didn't—until the service is over.

Kathryn Kuhlman's awareness that The Power has struck someone evidently is simultaneous with the healing itself.

In an instance reported by Dr. Robert Hoyt, the evangelist said from the platform: "A baby's deformed hip has just been healed." A mother in the service later testified that even as the words were being spoken she felt her baby's leg turn and the bones of his hip shift position.

In an instance which I personally observed, the simultaneity factor was dramatically evident. While she was praying for a man on the platform, Kathryn Kuhlman suddenly whirled and exclaimed: "Someone at the back is being healed of alcoholism at this moment!" While the words were being uttered—even before the sentence was complete—a young woman near me collapsed with a thud that resounded all over the auditorium. I was sure she had injured herself but, typically, she proved to have suffered not even a bruise.

Assisted by an usher, the woman went to the platform, gave her name and address, said that this was her first time in a miracle service and that, yes, she had indeed come to be healed of alcoholism.

The theory that Kathryn Kuhlman merely calls out a healing of a particular disease and waits for somebody to claim it is disproved by a number of facts. One is that the evangelist sometimes rejects candidates who think they are the one she meant ("No sir, it's not you; this is a woman"), and persists until she tracks down the target person.

"A man has just been healed of a back condition," I remember her saying once. "You're wearing a brace right now but you can take it off because you've been totally healed. Where are you?"

When no one responded, Kathryn Kuhlman proceeded to zero in, and it was astonishing to watch.

"You're in your fifties," she insisted. "You fell from a great height when you injured your back. You're on the right hand side on the ground floor. . . . Where are you? You feel a heat on your body. That's the Holy Spirit. You're sitting near the back on this side . . . the last six rows. . . . You're in that third row from the back. . . . *You,* sir."

The man she pinpointed, who appeared to be in his fifties, went to the platform and, somewhat sheepishly, admitted that what the evangelist had said about him was true, but that he had been too shy to respond. Kathryn

Kuhlman laughed, laid hands on him, and he promptly crumpled to the floor.

There are times when the evangelist's workers—most of them women who volunteer their services as a ministry—do pick out someone on their own and suggest that a healing being called out is for this particular person. There is reason to think that in some cases they may be mistaken. But, in many instances, that they are right is indicated by the reality of the healing. A case in point is Roy Lair.

Mr. Lair, a distinguished-looking man in his mid-forties who is an executive of a large Pittsburgh business corporation, developed, in April 1967, a condition which reduced him to semi-invalidism.

A hospital insurance report dated June 20, 1967, prepared by a neurologist, describes Mr. Lair's ailment as "infectious polyneuritis," or, literally, inflammation of many nerves. He underwent surgery to relieve pain and paralysis in his hands, said to be due to involvement of the nerves in the wrists. This condition is called, in the insurance document, "a bilateral carpal wrist tunnel syndrome." The nature of the surgical procedure is given as "excission of carpal tunnel ligaments, lysis disintegration of median nerves."

The operation left such deep scars in his wrists that Roy Lair quipped: "I looked as if I'd been stitched together like Frankenstein's monster."

His condition did not improve after the surgery, he said. He had serious doubts that he would ever get better. His wife was even more apprehensive because of some ominous news the doctor had given her.

"Before the operation Roy had been sent to a clinic in Cleveland," Mrs. Lair told me, "and our family doctor said to me the diagnosis was more serious than polyneuritis. He said that Roy had amytrophic lateral sclerosis [this will be defined shortly], the same thing that killed Lou Gehrig, and warned me that he would steadily deteriorate and within a few months would end up in a wheelchair.

"Now that Roy is better, the doctor says, 'Oh, our diagnosis must have been mistaken.' "

Depressed by his failure to respond to the operation, Roy Lair was open to any suggestion—even faith healing, something which he, as a respectable, middle-class Methodist, had never taken seriously. He heard of Kathryn Kuhlman through an Episcopal minister who believed in spiritual healing. So, in June 1967, the Lairs went to their first miracle service.

"Nothing happened," Mr. Lair said. "To me, that is. Oh, lots happened to other people. But frankly, I didn't know what to make of it—Kathryn Kuhlman calling out that somebody had been healed of cancer and a woman going up and saying it was her. I had no way of knowing whether she had really been healed or not. And all the people falling down when Miss Kuhlman prayed for them—it was dramatic all right, but I didn't know just what to make of it.

"However, there was something in that service that gripped me and made me determined to return."

At the second service Roy Lair got his questions answered.

"I was feeling worse. I had terrible pain and numbness in my leg, and my hands—which were still bandaged—were so dead that when I hit my finger I didn't feel it in my finger but all up my arm. My fingers were numb but the shock of any impact to them went right through me, as if I'd hit a piece of pipe.

"At the second service we sat in the fourth or fifth row from the front on the left side of the auditorium.

"The first thing Miss Kuhlman said when she came out

was, 'Someone over here has a spine condition, something to do with paralysis,' and she pointed in our direction. 'You're being healed right now,' she said.

"At that moment I had a sensation of extreme heat. One of the workers came up and said, 'Sir, that's for you. Claim it.' But I wanted to be sure it was real before I claimed anything. The worker insisted, and invited me to step out into the aisle. As I did so, I realized that the pain and stiffness in my leg had gone. And as I flexed and un-flexed my hands I knew that the pain and swelling in them seemed to have disappeared too.

"The rest is hazy. I know I went up on the platform and Miss Kuhlman prayed for me. What happened then I have no recollection of. All I remember is waking up on the floor and feeling wonderful. And I've felt wonderful ever since. Not only am I physically fine but my whole purpose in life has been deepened. I know now that God cares and that miracles do happen."

Mrs. Lair's description of what happened to her husband, as she saw it, is interesting.

"I don't think Roy realizes what actually did occur," she said. "Even before Miss Kuhlman spoke, he started shaking and turned deep red. I was shocked. I thought he was taking a heart attack. Then I must have gone into shock myself. I remember that worker speaking to him and Roy going up on the platform, but it's vague. One thing is defi-nite, though—he was healed."

Notice that Kathryn Kuhlman looked in the Lairs' direc-tion and said: "Someone over here has a spine condition, something to do with paralysis." A medical dictionary describes amytrophic lateral sclerosis as "muscular degen-eration and spinal cord degeneration." Could Kathryn Kuhlman have deduced this condition merely from the fact that Roy Lair was wearing bandages on his hands?

There are people who for some reason find Kathryn Kuhlman's strange diagnostic power harder to swallow than the fact of miraculous healings. But surely one strengthens the credibility of the other. As a matter of fact, it was just such odd features as instant diagnosis which convinced me in the first place that Kathryn Kuhlman's ministry had something to it. Niels Bohr, the great nuclear physicist, once said to a colleague: "Your theory is crazy but not crazy enough to be true." Kathryn Kuhlman's ministry *is* crazy enough—idiosyncratic, implausible, uninventable enough—to be true.

No matter how serious an affliction may be, if Kathryn Kuhlman receives the assurance that it's being healed, it generally is. Sometimes persons *in extremis* are brought back from the threshold of death.

I saw a man, said to be suffering from terminal stomach cancer, carried into the service by a pair of husky friends who had brought him from a hospital bed over the objections of the doctors. This man was unbelievably emaciated. During the meeting Kathryn Kuhlman announced that somebody with advanced cancer was being healed. A man, she said, on the ground floor to her left, near the back.

Suddenly the emaciated man began to vibrate as if he had touched a live wire. In a matter of moments he was standing unsupported.

The sequel: I saw this man in the next miracle service a week later. He obviously had gained a lot of weight (he said twenty-five pounds), looked fit, and demonstrated his well-being by doing pushups in the aisle. He said he had gone home from the miracle service and eaten voraciously. Ever since he had had "the appetite and digestion of a goat." The two friends who had carried him into the previous service, and his wife, confirmed this testimony.

Kathryn Kuhlman has told me that when she is "in the

Spirit" she often is shocked "when I hear myself say, 'This
person is healed of cancer,' or 'That person is being healed
of a club foot.' Of myself, I'd never dare say such things.
I'd be scared to death, in the natural sense. But when the
power of the Holy Spirit is on me, what happens isn't
natural but supernatural."

The evangelist deliberately avoids reading or hearing
about the various diseases that are healed in her meetings.
She cheerfully admits an ignorance of medicine that is
profound. Her reason?

"Well," she said, "if I knew too much about some of
these diseases I might start thinking, 'Oh, that's too terrible
to be healed.' I'd create a block in my own thinking that
might prevent the healings. So I don't want to know anything about the diseases. That way I'm too ignorant on
the subject to know that a certain disease can't be healed,
and therefore it is healed!"

It is this ineffable confidence, born of perfect faith,
which gives Kathryn Kuhlman the temerity to go out on
limbs from which even other healers would shrink. Once,
confronted by a ten-year-old girl with a club foot, she
summoned Dr. Cecil Titus from the congregation.

"You've always wanted to see a miracle as it happens,"
she said. "Well, come and see this one."

Dr. Titus—who served in the oral surgery department
of Cleveland's St. Luke's Hospital for thirty-one years and
was latterly head of the department—told me what happened when he went to the platform.

"The little girl had a club foot, all right. It was twisted
under. As Miss Kuhlman prayed I saw that girl's foot come
out and straighten as beautifully as you please. It was a
miracle, yes. But I saw it happen."

In a way, Kathryn Kuhlman is magnificently naïve about
her healings. To her, the disappearance of a skin rash is as

wonderful as the regression of a tumor. She has no medical viewpoint on whether one thing is harder than the other. For her it is God who does both and both are miracles.

When she is "in the Spirit," it's obvious that she is receiving impressions which she then translates, sometimes falteringly, into words. "It's something in the back," she'll say, groping for the right phrasing, "something . . . something to do with the spine," a description which could apply to conditions as disparate as a broken back and amytrophic lateral sclerosis.

Mrs. Mognet, who lives in Vandergrift, Pennsylvania, where she has a jewelry store, was taken to her first miracle service in October 1966. She had, according to her doctor, a "terminal" case of lupus erythematosus. This is a mysterious disorder, a collagen disease—that is, one associated with disturbances of the connective tissues, such as those around the joints and arteries—which ultimately attacks the blood vessels of the skin, the liver, the pancreas, and other organs of the body. It may be chronic and undergo periods of remission, or it can be acute and fatal. In Mrs. Mognet's case, her daughter, Mrs. Sydney Ann Ray, with whom she lived, was told by the doctor, that "Your mother's condition is terminal, you know, so try to make her as comfortable as possible."

The first sign of the disease in Emily Mognet's case was the sudden emergence of diabetes. This proved to be the result of damage to her pancreas. She also had liver damage with resultant jaundice, and the telltale rash on the hands and face that accompanies lupus erythematosus.

The definitive diagnosis was made, Mrs. Mognet said, after a comprehensive examination at a Pittsburgh hospital which included bone marrow tests, considered to be conclusive in cases of this kind. She was placed under the care of an internist as well as her family physician. Her treat-

ment consisted of a severely restricted diet (for the diabetes) and a spectrum of medications (notably cortisone)
to control the other symptoms.

As Emily Mognet described it, life was hell.

"I was taking, oh, it was either twenty-eight or thirty-
four pills a day," she said. "Sydney remembers better than
I do because she practically nursed me.

"I was a yellow color, mixed with a dull gray. And my
eyes—they seemed to have no definite color to them. . . .
The whites and the pupils were both the same, very bland.

"I was very weak. And my skin was painfully sensitive,
very sore in certain areas."

Mrs. Ray said: "During the months mother was with
us, I could see her deteriorate before my eyes. When I
asked the doctor about it, I got the same reply, 'Your
mother is terminal, you know. You've got to expect this.'"

As a last resort, Emily Mognet decided to go to a
Kathryn Kuhlman miracle service.

"One day I asked Sydney if she'd take me to one of the
services," Mrs. Mognet said. "She replied with something
like, 'Mom, I don't know how to get there.' So I let it drop
for then. After all, I knew that if it had been a women's
club meeting or something she really wanted to go to, she'd
find it even if it were on a rooftop.

"Well, some friends were visiting us and I mentioned
to them that I felt if I could get to a miracle service I'd be
healed. They said they'd take me, and immediately Sydney
said, 'Well, I'm going along.'"

At the service, they sat on the ground floor of the
auditorium, on the right-hand side near the front. During
the meeting Kathryn Kuhlman pointed in Emily Mognet's
direction and said: "There's a healing of diabetes down
here on my left; it's a woman."

Mrs. Mognet felt this was meant for her. She went to the
platform, Kathryn Kuhlman laid hands on her, and "I went

down under The Power. Something went through me, that's all I can say. I woke up with a tremendous feeling of well-being and joy."

Mrs. Mognet and her daughter and their friends went directly from the miracle service to a restaurant where Emily—who was on a salt-free, sugar-free diet—ate steak with lots of salt on it and ended up with a piece of strawberry pie exploding with calories.

"I knew I'd been healed," she said. "I just knew it, deep inside me. It wasn't fanaticism or being foolhardy. I knew the diabetes and the lupus erythematosus and all the rest were gone.

"During that meal, Sydney reached across the table and took my hand and said, 'Mom, God just gave you back to me.'

"And I asked her, 'Sydney, why didn't you take me to the miracle service when I wanted you to?' And she said, 'I was afraid. I knew God could heal you, but I was afraid if it didn't happen you'd be worse off than you already were.'

"My only regret," said Emily Mognet, "is that I've got a full bottle of cortisone left over since my healing and I'm just Scotch enough to want to sell it to somebody but I can't find a buyer."

Then she laughed, and it was the laughter of a vital, happy woman.

To this day, Kathryn Kuhlman doesn't know what it was that Emily Mognet was healed of. In conversation with me she kept talking about "lupus something-or-other, some funny kind of thing." But it wasn't necessary for her to be able to pronounce the disease to pick Emily Mognet out of the crowd and tell her that she was healed, as indeed she was, if more than two years of a total remission of symptoms means healing.

What is Kathryn Kuhlman's uncanny diagnostic power?

How does she know, by what means, that this or that person in the congregation is being healed?

This faculty has been studied extensively by scientists, notably Dr. J. B. Rhine and his associates at the former Parapsychology Laboratory of Duke University. There are marked affinities between Kathryn Kuhlman's strange diagnostic powers and clairvoyance as the parapsychologists have come to know it.

The person receiving the clairvoyant impression is often in an altered state of consciousness. The experience may come during sleep as an especially vivid dream, or in hypnosis, or in a so-called trance, either light or deep. It may come in a daydream or reverie. At any rate, there is generally some degree of "dissociation"—that is, a shutting out of normal sensory perceptions.

Kathryn Kuhlman is in an altered state of consciousness during the miracle services. She talks about being at times "out of the body," of being caught up in a kind of mystical rapture in which she is unaware of her surroundings.

She confided to me once, when we were having lunch at the Bel Air Hotel in Beverly Hills: "There is a point where I become so sensitive to the Holy Spirit that I can go ten minutes and I can't tell you what I've called out or what I've said."

On another occasion she said: "I'm totally unprepared with anything to say when I walk out on that platform for a miracle service. It just comes out. Later, people will have to tell me what I said. I'm completely detached from everything that goes on in that place. To come back after the service is almost like bringing the soul back into the body again. It has nothing to do with spiritualism or anything like that. I can't explain it.

"It's a condition of yielding yourself completely. You put forth no effort yourself. Sometimes, it's as though I were actually looking on rather than participating in the service. I see myself and hear myself, and I'm shocked at the audacity of some of the things I say."

From these quotations it is clear that Kathryn Kuhlman is not in a normal state during the healing service. Much of what she says matches the classic descriptions by the great Christian mystics of their experiences. And much of it sounds like the experiences of psychics when they are in a receptive mood. All psychics agree that you cannot force the clairvoyant power; you merely "yield yourself completely," to use Kathryn Kuhlman's phrase, "you put forth no effort yourself."

Kathryn Kuhlman, who knows nothing about parapsychology as such (and, I'm sure, doesn't want to know anything) might object to the word trance in connection with herself. Yet, it is, despite its connotations of dark rooms and mediums, a good biblical word. It appears, among other places, in Acts 10:10, speaking of Peter: ". . . he fell into a trance and saw heaven open . . ."

(There is even evidence that on occasions Kathryn Kuhlman goes into a deep trance, a condition she spoke of to me as "a different kind of sleep . . . a funny kind of sleep." We will consider one of these occasions in a later chapter when we explore just what it is in Kathryn Kuhlman that makes her the catalyst or channel of the healing power.)

Moreover, parapsychologists have found that the person receiving the clairvoyant impression usually has no real idea where the information is coming from. It's true that some psychics of the Spiritualist persuasion habitually interpret the source of their impressions as departed spirits, just as Kathryn Kuhlman interprets the source of her impressions as the Holy Spirit. But this is interpretation after the fact. There is no empirical way the psychic can know where his impressions originate or how. "I just know," the typical psychic will admit, if pressed about how or why he knows. And, as we have seen, Kathryn Kuhlman merely says with a shrug and a smile: "I know, but how or why I couldn't pretend to say."

Again, the clairvoyant impression generally is just that —an impression. Some psychics "hear" words, but most have a feeling, or see images, which must then be interpreted into words. Thus, a famous psychic, Arthur Ford, once said to me: "I see a side of wood . . . oh, now I understand. It's a name . . . Woodside."

Kathryn Kuhlman apparently receives an impression which she must translate, sometimes falteringly: "It's something wrong with a spine. . . ." "There's something about an ear . . . it happened when you were a child . . ." She rarely uses medical terms except in the most elementary way.

For the evangelist, these times of being in touch with sources of knowledge beyond the normal are sacred, holy occasions, even awesome. She stresses this. Her greatest fear is that she might lose The Power of which she stands as much in awe today as when it was first manifested.

"I often pray that God will take me before this anointing lifts," she told me once, speaking of the times when The Power comes upon her.

On another occasion she allowed: "Do I fear losing The Power? There's a prayer that David prayed, his greatest prayer, and I echo it daily, 'Take not Thy Holy Spirit from me.'

"There isn't a day of my life—and I say this with heaven as my witness—that I don't pray, 'Father God, You can have my last living relative. You can take my last copper penny. Leave me with only one outfit to clothe my body and one pair of shoes. But take not Thy Holy Spirit from me.' "

On still another occasion, Kathryn Kuhlman said to me: "When I'm in that miracle service I'm a different person. Would you believe me if I told you that at such times I don't even associate the name Kathryn Kuhlman with myself. That's true.

"If somebody stops me on the street—as they sometimes do—and asks me to pray for their healing there and then, I feel that it's sacrilege. They don't realize that when the Holy Spirit is upon me I'm a different person—more than Kathryn Kuhlman."

When the evangelist speaks in these terms she is as solemn as it is possible for a human being to be. There is no levity here, nothing but the most profound and grave emotion. One imagines that without The Power Kathryn Kuhlman would not live long.

Parapsychologists have discovered a link between religious-mindedness and psychic powers. Most—not all—psychically gifted persons are deeply religious. There is something about the religious state of mind, at its best, which appears to release the most profound and creative forces of the psyche. Kathryn Kuhlman is a classic example.

There is another feature of the evangelist's strange power that matches what parapsychologists know about clairvoyance—it is not infallible.

A highly qualified physician, who is a devoted admirer of Kathryn Kuhlman, said to me: "When I first got to know her ministry I accepted at face value her interpretation that it is God Himself who directly communicates to her the information she comes out with in the services. Now, however, I've come to think that it is a form of ESP.

"The reason is that sometimes Miss Kuhlman is wrong. And if it were the Holy Spirit, I can't see that He could err."

This doctor cited two separate instances in which the

evangelist had pinpointed women in a miracle service and told them that they had breast cancer which was healed. On checking, the doctor found that Kathryn Kuhlman's diagnosis was correct. Both women, encouraged by the evangelist's assurance they had been healed, testified to this as fact. Both showed a dramatic improvement which lasted for a short time. And both died of cancer.

"In one case the woman had widespread metastasis [secondary malignant growths]," the doctor said. "Before the miracle service she had been bedridden for six months and was unable hardly to ride in a car. After the service she was able to walk and she lived normally for a month or more with no pain. And then suddenly the cancer came back. She deteriorated and died within five months."

However, the evidence suggests strongly that Kathryn Kuhlman's clairvoyance, as a rule, is remarkably accurate. And, in cases where apparent healing is followed by a relapse, there is no way of knowing whether or not the person actually did receive some unusual blessing but deteriorated because his psychological makeup predisposed him to a relapse. Maybe even God can't overcome the will to die in some people.

Of course, this is speculation. And it would not alter the fact that sometimes what the evangelist called healings ("And the person God heals stays healed," she's fond of saying) proved to be only temporary remissions.

There is no necessary incompatibility, in my mind, between Kathryn Kuhlman's profound belief that it is God who tells her these things and the view that the phenomenon is a form of clairvoyance. Even if the two were logically contradictory—which they are not—the principle of complementarity says that in physics two mutually contradictory facts (e.g., that light is made up of waves, and that it is made up of discrete particles) can both be true. In the realm of the psychic, even more than in physics, *A can equal non-A*.

There is nothing contradictory in saying that Kathryn Kuhlman's gift is clairvoyance, and, in the same breath, that it is due to the power of God. If, as theologians admit, it is God who heals, whether the cure comes by prayer, by penicillin, by surgery, by suggestion, or by a combination of any or all of them, why can we not say that it is God who speaks to Kathryn Kuhlman, whether immediately, as she feels, or through a psychic mechanism which we call clairvoyance?

The fact that occasionally her information is wrong no more invalidates its divine origin than the fact that some patients don't respond to medical treatment disproves the idea that healing can take place through medicine.

For myself, I am perfectly happy to say that Kathryn Kuhlman's ministry, viewed from one perspective, is a manifestation of the power of God if anything in this world is. In a more technical interpretation, I would be prepared to speculate that God expresses Himself through extra-sensory processes which, like everything else about man, are subject to error. The theologian might say that it is not God who errs when there is an "error," but man's interpretation.

There is no doubt in my mind that Kathryn Kuhlman is an instrument, a channel. Whether The Power that works through her is called God, the Holy Spirit, the Deep Mind, the Universal Unconscious, the Life Force, or whatever, doesn't alter the reality. Kathryn Kuhlman is the means by which miracles—wonderful things—happen.

But why? How did it start? How does it happen?

These are questions we will now consider.

11

The Coming of The Power

"How did my healing ministry start? That's a good question," Kathryn Kuhlman said, sipping her coffee.

We were chatting in the evangelist's well-appointed offices—which include a small but fully equipped radio and recording studio—in Pittsburgh's Carlton House Hotel. She was in an uncharacteristic, relaxed mood, reminiscing about her ministry and how the miracles began.

"The very first miracle was in . . . well, let's see . . . it was 1946." As she talked, the evangelist toyed with the long string of beads around her neck.

"I was preaching in Franklin, Pennsylvania. One night my sermon was on the Holy Spirit. I hadn't mentioned healing. But the next night, before I began to preach, a woman stood up and said, 'Pardon me Miss Kuhlman, but I have a testimony to give. While you were preaching last night I had a strange sensation in my body and I knew I had been healed. I knew it. Today I went to my doctor and he confirmed that I was.'

"As I recollect, the woman had had a tumor. And that was the beginning, the first of the miracles."

That event divided Kathryn Kuhlman's ministry into two distinct phases: before the coming of The Power, and after.

In the first phase she was just another itinerant evangelist, a little more eloquent and energetic than most, perhaps, but otherwise undistinguished. In some twenty years of preaching she had whistle-stopped her way across the American Midwest several times ("I bet I preached in every little church in Idaho," she quipped).

The second phase of her ministry was a much different story. That initial healing was the start of an unbroken succession. Word spread about the woman evangelist who worked miracles. The sick began to make pilgrimages to her services. She took to the air waves, and the crowds grew larger still. Since then there has been no turning back.

What led to the extraordinary event which the evangelist and her followers speak of as "the coming of The Power"?

Kathryn Kuhlman is a very private person when it comes to talking about her personal life. This is not to suggest that she is evasive; indeed, I have found her to be disarmingly candid about certain aspects of her life (her educational inadequacies, for example). But since she does apparently think of her life since the coming of The Power as radically different from what it was before, events from that earlier period seem to have receded more than normally into the back of her mind.

Of this dichotomy in her life, she has said: "If I were to tell you that I don't even associate that name Kathryn Kuhlman with myself, I tell you the truth. In a real sense, Kathryn Kuhlman is dead."

This is a fascinating statement, one that was spoken with the most intense emotion possible. It hints at the complexity and depth of this unusual woman, and conveys a sense of the total, radical change in her life that was made by the coming of that Power—a change so profound that, for her, I am convinced, talking about the first part of her life is like talking about a person who is dead.

Kathryn Kuhlman was born in the small town (population 1,200) of Concordia, Missouri. The date is classified. (Like many women, she would rather be put to torture than reveal her age. In my book *The Unexplained* I mention that the evangelist says she is eighty-four, an obviously —or so I thought—facetious remark. Many readers, however, took me seriously. One woman wrote to say that she had seen a picture of the evangelist, "and if she's really eighty-four and looks like that, that's the biggest miracle of all!" A doctor wrote demanding to know who the "imposter" was who was holding meetings in Pittsburgh under Kathryn Kuhlman's name. "You say she's eighty-four," he explained, "and this woman can't be a day over thirty-five." Let me say here that Kathryn Kuhlman, as she herself put it in a letter to an inquirer, is "a long way from eighty-four." Beyond that, my lips are sealed.)

Her father, says Kathryn Kuhlman, was mayor of Concordia. "I was not," she said, "brought up in a deeply religious home." In fact, she remembers her father as having "a deep aversion to preachers—so deep that if he saw one coming he'd cross the street to avoid meeting him."

But young Kathryn loved her father. In fact, every time I've heard her talk about her childhood the remark recurs like a litany: "I loved my poppa more than anything else in the world."

As she describes herself, the evangelist must have been quite a girl.

"I would never take anyone's word for anything," she says with that husky laugh so familiar to those who know her. "I had to find out for myself. Once I plugged every watermelon in my grandpa's watermelon patch full of holes trying to find out if one of them wasn't purple."

On another memorable occasion, Kathryn went around the neighborhood inviting some thirty women to a birthday party for her mother with the stipulation that each bring a cake. Her mother knew nothing about it until the mob converged on her house one afternoon, all bearing cakes. Retribution, as the evangelist recalls, was swift and acutely unpleasant.

When she was almost fourteen a climactic event occurred.

"It was one Sunday morning, when I was in the little Methodist church that seats not more than a hundred people," Kathryn Kuhlman said.

"I cannot tell you what the preacher said at that service, or what hymns were sung. But suddenly something happened to me. It's as real to me right now as it was then— the most real thing that had ever happened to me.

"I began to tremble. This was my very first experience of the Holy Spirit. Suddenly I felt like the meanest, lowest person in the whole world. I trembled so violently I couldn't hold the hymn book. It was my first contact with the power of God. I sat down in the pew and sobbed. Nobody in the church knew what was wrong with me. But something wonderful had happened.

"On the way home from church everything looked brighter, more beautiful. My feet didn't touch the sidewalk. Then suddenly I knew what it was: Jesus had come into my heart. There was no doubt in my mind after that. I knew that I knew that I knew. That was the beginning of everything."

Perhaps it would be more accurate, in terms of Kathryn Kuhlman's later career, to say that her conversion was the beginning of the beginning. And the beginning—the

phase of her ministry preceding the coming of The Power
—lasted for a number of years.

She preached her first sermon when she was fifteen. "It
was on Zaccheus up the tree," she recalled with a chuckle,
"and if ever anybody was up a tree, I was."

Kathryn Kuhlman was a school dropout. This makes her
subsequent achievements even more remarkable.

"For years I had a complex because I've got no degrees
or seminary training," she has said. "All I know is what
I've learned as I've watched the Holy Spirit at work."

That, of course, has turned out to be quite enough.

It would be a mistake to think of Kathryn Kuhlman as
intellectually dull. She is about as dull as a rapier.

I have often thought, as I watched her: "This woman is
nobody's fool." Anyone trying to impose on her would
speedily discover that she is both keen-minded and, if the
occasion requires, tough-minded. In a conflict over a matter
of principle she could be a redoubtable foe, as forceful as
any man.

The evangelist has a framed poster, yellowed with the
years, on her office wall. It shows a photograph of a very
young woman, still in her teens, her hair a mass of curls
and her pretty features illuminated by a dazzling smile.
The poster bears an announcement that evangelist Kathryn
Kuhlman will be preaching at revival services and all are
invited to hear her expound on the word of God.

"In those days I used to sleep in turkey houses if there
was nothing better," Kathryn Kuhlman told me. "I had no
money. It was an event when I got fifteen cents to buy a
pair of lisle stockings."

Along the way the evangelist picked up converts. Once,
she gave up one-night stands on the revival circuit to
pastor a church in Denver.

Throughout this part of her ministry she was aware of

"a deep hunger for more of God." She wondered why the power which had accompanied the preaching of the Gospel in the early days of Christianity wasn't visible now. Why, for example, weren't the sick healed? She attended many services where prayer was offered for the sick but something always was missing.

"For one thing, I saw many sick people prayed for but I didn't see any healed. You don't need much mentality, after all, to tell if somebody is really healed.

"And I knew why the evangelist asked people to fill out those cards to get in the healing line. It was to get a mailing list, that's all. I used to sit there and watch this kind of thing and I wasn't satisfied that it was real. I knew this wasn't what I was looking for. Yet I knew there was something to it, that miracles could take place today just as in the Bible. But I didn't know how."

She still doesn't know how, in so many words. But she knows *when* miracles started for her personally. They followed the most electrifying religious experience of her life, and this came after a deep personal tragedy.

"I had a sorrow, I had a heartbreak," she has said about that time in her life.

"I remember walking down a dead-end street and realizing that my life was a dead-end street. It was four o'clock on a Saturday afternoon. It was at that time and in that place that I surrendered myself fully to the Holy Spirit.

"There are some things too sacred to talk about. I will only say that in that moment, with tears streaming down my face, God and I made each other promises. He knows that I'll be true to Him and I know that I'll be true to Him. In that moment, I yielded to God in body, soul, and spirit. I gave him everything.

"Then I knew what the scripture meant about taking up your cross. A cross is the symbol of death. That afternoon,

Kathryn Kuhlman died. And when I died, God came in, the Holy Spirit came in. There, for the first time, I realized what it meant to have power."

It was after this overwhelming mystical experience that Kathryn Kuhlman started preaching specifically on the power of the Holy Spirit. The experience brought with it a kind of self-surrender, a radical selflessness, which she had not felt before. God became so real to her that the mundane world receded into a relative unreality. The immediacy of her perception of God was so overpowering that at times she felt it was God controlling her body, not she herself.

"Without the Holy Spirit, I'm sunk," Kathryn Kuhlman says. "I know better than anybody else that apart from Him I have nothing. No education. No talents. Nothing.

"In the miracle services, when I walk out on that platform I die a thousand deaths. The longest walk I ever take is the walk from the wings to behind that pulpit. The reason I walk so fast is because I can hardly wait for the anointing of the Holy Spirit to come upon me."

And what happens when the Holy Spirit "comes upon" her?

This is the out-of-the-body experience which has been alluded to earlier. This is the altered state of consciousness in which Kathryn Kuhlman is caught up in mystic rapture. This is the ecstasy in which I have seen her, at times, stand for several minutes, in what appears to be a cataleptic state, her face upturned, her hands outstretched in prayer, unmoving, transfixed, an ethereal smile on her lips. She seems oblivious of her surroundings, in a transport of wonder and of joy.

"I'm completely detached from everything that goes on in that place," Kathryn Kuhlman told me. "It's as if my body is possessed by the Holy Spirit. It's as though I were removed, up above somewhere, looking down on the proceedings. I see myself, and I'm shocked when I hear myself say things like, 'A cancer is being healed.'

"I'm a bystander looking on and as amazed as anyone else by the miracles. And I'm having the time of my life. If nobody else enjoys the service, I do! I love every minute of it.

"I'm glad I'm stupid. I'm just as amazed as anybody else in the auditorium at what's happening. And I know that I have nothing to do with it. As the Bible says, 'Not by might, not by power, but by My Spirit, saith the Lord.'"

The first physical miracle, the healing of the woman with a tumor, was a prototype of the thousands to follow. The same features recurred later: The woman had been healed while sitting in her pew; she felt a "strange sensation" in her body; the healing apparently was quasi-instantaneous.

The second miracle was the case of George Orr, the man who received sight in his blind eye after twenty-seven years. He too, you remember, was healed where he sat and felt a "tingling sensation" in the eye.

Kathryn Kuhlman pondered the mystery behind these miracles which had come unbidden and unexpected. What caused them?

"I realized that it was the presence of the Holy Spirit," she said. "When the power of the Spirit is there, miracles happen.

"Gradually, I began to understand The Power, how it operates. I discovered that certain things bring the presence of the Holy Spirit. Praise, for instance. Just praising God —not asking for a single thing but just praising Him—always brings The Power. It's pleasing to the Lord."

The evangelist is very sensitive, however, to any suggestion that The Power can be used, as if it were the secret

ent in a new brand of toothpaste or a wonder drug
ken three times a day.

You do not manipulate the Holy Spirit," she declaims
with vehemence. "The Holy Spirit is a person. He is not an
it. He is God. He is to be reverenced, to be worshiped. He
is not to be presumed upon by anyone."

Word of the miracles spread and the sick began to flock
to the little church in Franklin, Pennsylvania. Soon the
crowds were too large to be accommodated. This is when
the evangelist decided to move her base of operations to
Pittsburgh.

"I began in Pittsburgh on the Fourth of July, 1947,"
she mused.

"I remember dreaming the night before that nobody
came. I still have that dream. To this very day, there is
never a service but what I am amazed that anybody shows
up.

"We rented the city-owned Carnegie Auditorium for two
weeks. I remember asking that extra folding chairs be put
on the platform and the custodian said, 'You will not need
folding chairs because nobody ever gets a crowd in this
place.'

"When I got there the next day the place was packed to
the rafters. It was packed three hours before the service."

The original two weeks stretched into six months of services—one every night of the week—in Carnegie Auditorium. There were complaints from a few people, said
Kathryn Kuhlman, that she was turning the city-owned auditorium into a church. But Pittsburgh's mayor (later state
governor), David Lawrence, a Catholic as it happens, was
her staunch friend and supporter. He issued instructions
that Kathryn Kuhlman was to stay in Carnegie Auditorium
as long as she wanted.

She stayed for twenty years, until plans for renovation

and remodeling of the building were put into effect. Then she moved the miracle services to their present location, the spacious, fashionable First Presbyterian Church in downtown Pittsburgh.

Some of the early healings remain landmarks in the Kuhlman ministry.

In May 1949, Mary Schmidt, of Pittsburgh, received instant healing of a massive goiter. A tremendous "Oh" went up from the congregation as the lump on Mrs. Schmidt's neck melted away. Today you can see her at any miracle service—still minus the goiter.

A Pittsburgh policeman, Paul Gunn, came into his first miracle service hobbling on two crutches. He was dying of lung cancer. That was in October 1949. During a service a few weeks later, Paul Gunn felt a sudden surge of heat shoot through his chest and he was healed. For skeptics he keeps a copy of his medical records.

Dolly Graham, also from Pittsburgh, was healed of a terminal heart condition while Kathryn Kuhlman prayed. Mrs. Graham was an adult version of a blue baby, but suddenly turned pink "as though a blood transfusion were taking place," reported her sister-in-law, Mrs. Elizabeth Gethin, a nurse who witnessed the healing.

Stella Turner, from Masillon, Ohio, was so riddled with cancer that the surgeons simply sewed her up again, telling her husband it was pointless to operate. She vomited continuously on the way to her first miracle service in Youngstown, Ohio. But at that service, "I felt The Power," she says. Within a few weeks she was eating normally. That was twenty years ago.

Healings of alcoholism became commonplace. Today the Kathryn Kuhlman men's choir includes many members who were once pathological drinkers. Healings of drug addiction, too, have been reported. One case, that of "Rose" (a fictitious name), a teen-aged girl from a good family who got hooked on narcotics, was extraordinary because the addiction vanished instantly. Such a change requires not only a psychological convulsion but the erasing of an actual physiological need.

Kathryn Kuhlman's favorite healing—in the sense that of them all it remains the most vividly etched in her mind —was that of Billie Fischer, a hydrocephalic baby, she told me.

When Billie (a girl) was ten months old, the diagnosis of hydrocephalus—"water on the brain"—was made by one of Pittsburgh's leading neurosurgeons at the Allegheny General Hospital. With Mrs. Fischer's permission, I gained access to the hospital records. They confirm that the child was hydrocephalic. The prognosis was "guarded." (A medical informant tells me this is a euphemism for "grave.")

Mrs. Fischer said that several doctors advised her to place the child in an institution for incurables. The mother refused and took her to Kathryn Kuhlman's services.

The evangelist well remembers "the little waterhead baby." How could she forget her? It was the first case of hydrocephalus she had seen and the monstrous swelling of the child's head appalled her. The mother kept the baby shrouded in a blanket so as not to repel those sitting nearby in the services.

After the first service the child improved and continued to improve. Surgery, which the doctors said was imperative to tap the fluid on the brain, was not performed. In a few weeks the child's appearance was normal. Today she is a perfectly healthy and charming young lady.

Was this a "spontaneous remission?" (These are the words which some doctors invoke too readily to conjure away any healing they can't explain.)

Well, the comment of an obstetrician was: "Not likely. Especially in a case where the prognosis was guarded. Remissions of hydrocephalus can happen, apparently. But in all the cases I've come across in my practice—and they run into the scores—I can't think of a single spontaneous remission."

Another healing which sticks out particularly in Kathryn Kuhlman's memory happened recently. For some reason, it impressed her in a similar, vivid way as did the case of hydrocephalus. The person healed, in early 1966, was an elderly man named Charles Bokach, who lives in a suburb of Pittsburgh.

"Of all the people who've been healed in the miracle services," said Kathryn Kuhlman, "I can't remember anyone who sobbed as this man did. It was as though his heart was breaking."

Mr. Bokach had a growth on his ear, a disfiguring mass that the doctor suspected was cancerous. Final tests were ordered; if this diagnosis was confirmed, Mr. Bokach faced having all or part of his ear amputated.

He went forward for prayer at a miracle service. The evangelist recalls that his ear was grotesquely swollen and a foul discharge had soaked through the bandage on it.

Suddenly, to Kathryn Kuhlman's amazement, the ear appeared normal. It was as sudden as that. The bandage was removed and no trace of the suppurating wound remained. Indeed, the top half of the ear—as I was able to confirm for myself not long after the healing—was as pink as a newborn baby's, as though made of fresh tissue.

This instant and highly visible healing staggered the evangelist, whom one might expect to be somewhat blasé about miracles after twenty years of watching them.

Kathryn Kuhlman confesses that through the years she has been surprised, amazed, amused, and sometimes

shaken up by the curious ways in which The Power operates.

"I've decided that God doesn't have preferences in
theology," she told me with a chuckle. "We are the ones
who try to put a fence around God, to bring Him down to
our level. But it doesn't work. God is too big for us to
confine.

"I've never written a book on the how and why of divine
healing—even though I've been besieged with requests to
do so—simply because I *don't know* the how or why.

"You see, just about the time the book was to be published, the Holy Spirit would do something absolutely con-
trary to what I had said. I'm still learning the mysterious
ways in which God moves. I'll tell you one thing—I'm sure
God has a sense of humor!"

Some of her own theological presuppositions have been
shattered, the evangelist allows.

"There was a day, when I was very young and knew a
great deal more than I do now, that I said, 'You must do
thus and so to be healed. There are certain conditions that
have to be met.' I thought, for example, that faith on the
part of the seeker was absolutely necessary.

"Then one day I got the shock of my life. A man said
his deaf ear had just been opened in a service, but he had
no faith at all. 'I don't believe in it,' he said. 'I never go to
church.' Well, there went my theology out the window.

"Another time, a young woman who was healed of a
spinal condition admitted that right up to the moment of
her healing the only emotion she felt was annoyance and
anger at me, for some reason. But she was healed. The
shock almost scared her to death! Changed her attitude,
too.

"Take another example. Twenty years ago I believed
that absolutely, come hell or high water, it was God's will

for everybody, without exception, to be healed. But I've watched this thing very carefully. Now I see that we can't demand or command that God do anything. In general I definitely believe that it is God's will to heal. But I can't say absolutely what is or is not His will in a particular case. There are some things I've learned just not to touch."

Kathryn Kuhlman, it occurred to me, is not unlike the famous artist Jackson Pollock, who used to create his celebrated dribble paintings in an unconscious, dreamlike state, and only after he was finished, would stand back to look at what he had wrought and say, "Well, what do you know!"

She puts it inimitably in her nonstop, stream-of-consciousness prose: "Sometimes in the miracle service I stand there and I see all these wonderful things happen and I don't understand *how* they happened or what happened to cause them to happen, and all I know is that we made contact someplace but I don't know how, and if we were just smart enough to know *how* we made contact. . . . Well . . . I feel so stupid sometimes."

One of the features of the miracle services that intrigued her early was the clustering of healings in particular areas of the auditorium. Was there a sort of contagion in the healings, as though health as well as sickness could be caught?

"There will be a part of the auditorium where suddenly The Power falls, and six or seven people are healed right in a group," the evangelist said.

"This has shown me that there is a spiritual force released when people's hearts are united. The glory falls when a group, in the words of the Book of Acts, 'are all with one accord in one place.' I have nothing to do with this. It's their own power in prayer, their oneness in the Spirit."

Sometimes the evangelist will announce a healing and add: "The people sitting near that person are getting the overflow from the healing. The Power's right there now. Take your own healing, quickly!"

Such language suggests that The Power is what physicists call a "field phenomenon" (a field is defined as a "model for representing the way in which a force can exist between two bodies not in contact"). Presumably this would be similar to an electric or magnetic field.

All sorts of questions come to mind. If this hypothetical healing force field really exists, what is its nature—physical or nonphysical? What is its source? Kathryn Kuhlman? Or is the congregation as a whole a kind of giant magnet and Kathryn Kuhlman only a catalyst, so to speak? How far does the healing field extend?

Some scientific research has been performed that is pertinent to such questions. Previous mention was made of the work of Dr. Bernard Grad, a biologist at Montreal's McGill University, who set out to determine whether or not prayer could actually influence cell growth in plants and animals. In his experiments he worked with a man named Oskar Estebany, a retired Hungarian army colonel now living in Montreal, who claimed he had a healing gift which emanated from his hands and manifested itself in a therapeutic effect on sick people, animals, and even plants.

To test Mr. Estebany's claims, Dr. Grad devised a simple experiment. Twenty-four peat pots were filled with soil, and twenty barley seeds were planted in each. The pots were divided into two equal groups at random; one the experimental group and the other the control one. Instead of having the subject hold his hands over the plants as he prayed, Grad gave him a sealed bottle of saline solution (water with 1 percent salt added) in which to try to impregnate his healing force. This solution was then poured over the experimental plants. The effect of the salt was to make the plants "sick," thus increasing the significance of any detected benefit from the prayer. The plants in the control group got only "untreated" (not-prayed-over) saline solution. Otherwise, the two groups received identical care.

The experiment lasted fourteen days. Results? The plants that had received the prayed-over solution grew significantly taller and more robust than those in the control group.

This basic experiment was repeated many times by Dr. Grad, with a progressive tightening of controls to rule out conventional explanations (the double-blind method, for example, was introduced, in which neither Dr. Grad nor Mr. Estebany knew which group of plants was receiving the prayed-over solution—a third experimenter recorded this). The results were consistently positive; in every experiment the plants watered with the prayed-over solution grew faster and became more robust than those in the control group.

Another series of tests on the "prayer effect" involved mice. Three groups of these animals were given wounds on their backs made by surgically removing an area of skin. These areas were then measured over an eighteen-day period. The first group of mice received prayer and handling each day from Mr. Estebany. The second group received prayer and handling from a number of different individuals who claimed no healing power. The third group was given neither prayer nor handling.

The results showed significantly faster healing in the first group of mice—the one that received prayer and handling from the healer—than in the other two groups.

(The reader who is interested in the full technical details of Dr. Grad's experiments should consult the more

complete account in my book *The Unexplained,* or the
original report in the *International Journal of Parapsychology,* vol. 3, no. 2, 1961.)

Dr. Grad summed up the significance of his research in
an interview with me. "Apparently there is a power released by prayer," he said. "It is an actual force. It pene-
trates the glass jar in which the water is; therefore we
know it is not some chemical factor like sweat or breath.
It is an energy—something that moves.

"Some people can generate this force which is capable
of stimulating cell growth in plants and animals. I know
of no conventional force that will act both on plant and
animal growth as this prayer force apparently does. Neither
electricity nor magnetism acts in this way."

These experiments indicate that a healing force can
impregnate a substance—such as water—and be transmitted through that medium. Interestingly, there is evidence that Lourdes water, although chemically not different
from any other spring water in that part of France, has
the power of rendering virulent germs inert. Dr. François
Leuret, President of the Lourdes Medical Bureau, said that
experiments at the Naples Institute of Hygiene have shown
that animals injected with microbes subjected to Lourdes
water do not develop disease, but similar animals injected
with microbes subjected to the water of a local river die
within a few days. Apparently, then, germs lose their
virulence as soon as they come in contact with Lourdes
water. Yet, as I've said, there is no known chemical basis
for this.[1]

One theory is that, over the period of more than a century that Lourdes has been a shrine, its water has become
charged with healing force by the prayers of millions of

---

[1] The phenomenon is reported in *A Doctor Heals by Faith* by Christopher Woodard, Max Parrish, London, 1959.

pilgrims. Today that water is, evidently, psychically radioactive, giving off therapeutic emanations which are not detectable by any instrument known to science.

There is a biblical parallel for this sort of phenomenon. Acts 19, verses 11 and 12 read: "And God wrought special miracles by the hands of Paul: So that from his body were brought unto the sick handkerchiefs or aprons, and the disease departed from them . . ." Apparently, a healing force from Paul's body was transmitted through the cloths. No other interpretation seems to fit this passage.

Research by scientists has uncovered possible bodily mechanisms in healing, and certain similarities between the healing force and some conventional forms of radiation.

Sister M. Justa Smith, Chairman of the Chemistry Department at Rosary Hill College in Buffalo, New York, heard of the research by Dr. Grad (and other pioneers in prayer-on-plant research, notably Rev. Franklin Loehr), and decided to test the prayer effect on enzymes. The study of enzymes is Sister Justa's special field; her Ph.D. research was in the effects of ultraviolet light and high magnetic fields upon enzyme activity.

Enzymes play a vital part in health. They are the catalysts which regulate all the metabolic reactions of every body cell. In fact, enzymes are so important that they are referred to by biochemists as the "brains" of the cells.

It would seem to follow, or so Sister Justa felt, that any disease or illness proceeds from a lack of, or malfunctioning of, some enzyme. And any change from sickness to health would require a prior change in the enzymes.

Sister Justa set up, then, the following hypothesis: "Any healing force channeled through or activitated by the hands of an unorthodox healer must affect enzyme activity if healing is to take place." To test the hypothesis, she performed a series of experiments working with the same Mr. Estebany.

The model of the experiments was simple enough. Choosing an enzyme called trypsin, Sister Justa proposed to compare any effects from Mr. Estebany's hands with those produced by ultraviolet light and magnetic fields.

Every day during the period of experimentation four bottles of trypsin solution were prepared. The first received no treatment. The second was held in Mr. Estebany's hands for seventy-five minutes while he prayed over it. The third was irradiated by ultraviolet light, which is known to reduce the enzyme's activity by 60 to 80 percent, and then held and prayed for by Mr. Estebany. The fourth solution was exposed to a high magnetic field for periods of up to four hours.

The results of these experiments, said Sister Justa, indicated greatly increased activity of the treated enzymes compared with the untreated or control solutions.

The activity of the enzyme in bottles held by Mr. Estebany was comparable to that obtained in a high magnetic field. Also, the rate of activity in the "damaged" enzymes, which had been exposed to ultraviolet radiation, returned to normal after being held by Mr. Estebany.

Sister Justa said: "It is interesting to note that the qualitative effect of a high magnetic field and of the hands of this healer are the same; and they are also quantitatively similar up to one hour of exposure." In other words, not only did enzyme activity increase after magnetic radiation and treatment by Mr. Estebany, respectively, but in both cases the rate of increase over a sixty-minute period was nearly the same.

A British barrister named Eric Cuddon, who claims success in relieving pain by the laying on of hands, speculates that the phenomenon has an electrical basis and involves a "restoration of electrostatic balance."

Similarities in the effects produced by magnetism, static electricity, and the healing force do not necessarily indicate that the latter is an electromagnetic phenomenon. Similar effects may proceed from dissimilar causes. Blisters on the skin, for example, might be caused by things as disparate as direct sunlight, a mustard poultice, and sulphuric acid.

However, J. Stephen Ogden, a chemist with the Ashland Oil and Refining Company in Ashland, Kentucky, thinks that "ESP waves," in which he includes the healing force, may yet be found to be part of the electromagnetic spectrum—in other words, to be a physical radiation.

Mr. Ogden's intriguing theory is that "chemicals are the basic cause of disease, whether it be a crippled leg, eye trouble, ear trouble, or mental problems. When considering the chemical effects in the body one must remember that all chemical reactions involve a passage of electricity. Magnetism is, of course, intimately involved with electrical phenomena.

"With what I have learned about how chemicals which disturb body functions are added and removed, none of the cures by Kathryn Kuhlman seem strange to me. The flow of negative electrons from a powerful 'magnetic' personality like hers enables the body to remove the chemicals that cause disease. The calcifications of arthritis are insoluble chemical compounds of calcium which are rapidly made soluble by the flow of negative electrons. The calcification is formed in the first place by negatively charged radicals which form *positive* electrons."

On the other hand, Dr. Grad doubts that the healing force is an electromagnetic phenomenon. Although his own experiments ended before this question could be settled, he points to tests by other parapsychologists indicating that ESP—including psychokinesis, or the direct action of mind on matter, which presumably includes healing—is not physical in nature.

The Russian parapsychologist, the late L. L. Vasiliev, reported an experiment with telepathy where the subject was enclosed in a lead-lined cabinet which was then immersed in a mercury bath. The subject apparently received a telepathic transmission, although no known electromagnetic radiation can penetrate lead or mercury, much less both combined.

In an experiment with the "psychic photographer" Ted Serios, at the University of Colorado, Serios was seated inside a Faraday Cage—a chamber designed to screen out electromagnetic phenomena—while the camera was triggered by a scientist outside. Serios successfully imprinted a mental image on the photographic film. He also was successful in producing pictures from his mind when separated from the camera by a shield of lead-impregnated glass, such as is used to protect X-ray technicians from harmful radiation.[2]

One of the cardinal tenets of Dr. J. B. Rhine, the high priest of parapsychologists, is the "nonphysicality" of ESP.

How far then does the hypothetical healing field extend in space? In the case of Kathryn Kuhlman, it appears at least to overflow the immediate boundaries of the auditorium in which the miracle service is being held. One woman told me of her experience: "I was walking up the steps outside the building when, wham, down I went. A man helped me up and said, 'Are you all right? Don't

[2] Fuller details of the Serios phenomenon can be found in *The World of Ted Serios* by Jules Eisenbud, William Morrow & Co., Inc., New York, 1967; and in my book *The Unexplained*.

worry, that was the power of God.' Then I realized that the arthritis I'd had in my hands for years was gone. I'd been healed and I wasn't even in the service yet!"

Another woman reported that she and her husband drove from Philadelphia to Pittsburgh to attend a miracle service, after she had read about Kathryn Kuhlman. The woman was suffering from acute emphysema, an incurable lung disease that can be fatal. As she stepped through the door into the auditorium, she collapsed. When she came to, she found she was healed of her emphysema. The woman's husband corroborated her story.

Now, some observers would argue that the most likely explanation for this kind of behavior is suggestion or hysteria; these women knew what to expect and their unconscious minds gave it to them. However, that doesn't explain their healings. Arthritis does not respond instantly to suggestion, even when powerful emotion is involved, and emphysema causes structural changes in the lungs which suggestion could hardly influence so suddenly and dramatically. Moreover, in both cases the remission of symptoms lasted at least a period of several months, for it was that long after the healings when I talked to the women.

Kathryn Kuhlman tells a funny story about The Power which settled any momentary uncertainty that she may have had about whether it was a form of "mass hypnosis," as some critics argued.

"When we first went to Los Angeles for services," she said, "I was curious to see what would happen where people didn't know much, if anything, about The Power and how it works.

"Well, at one service there were fifty Marines who were soon going to Vietnam. I invited them to the platform for special prayer. As I laid hands on the first one—down he went! And so did the others, like a row of ten pins. Now, brother, it takes more than the power of suggestion to bowl over fifty U.S. Marines!"

The lady may have a point.

Can The Power operate at considerable distances from the evangelist?

Kathryn Kuhlman told me a story that sheds light on this question. Because of certain peculiar circumstances, it seems impossible to say that the healing in this story definitely was caused by the force field I've postulated. But it is a curious and fascinating incident which includes what seems to have been the phenomenon of collective trance.

On July 11, 1957, Robert Byers, a twenty-one-year-old student from Grove City College, Pennsylvania, was suddenly taken ill on his summer construction job in Newfoundland. Doctors at the nearby U.S. Naval Dispensary diagnosed his illness as Guillain Barre Syndrome, a form of polyneuritis similar to polio, and with a high death rate.

The student was flown to a hospital in Boston which had facilities for the special treatment he needed. He arrived in critical condition, with virtually total paralysis. From July to October he oscillated between life and death, the whole period a medical phantasmagoria of tracheotomies, iron lungs, blood transfusions, and lung punctures.

Kathryn Kuhlman entered the story when Robert Byers was scheduled for massive lung surgery, the most serious crisis he had yet faced. His family learned of the pending operation on the weekend of October 19. His parents contacted the evangelist, asking her to come to Boston and pray for him. She replied that she could pray just as well in Pittsburgh, and set one o'clock on the following Friday as the time for special prayers on his behalf. She asked his family to pray for him at exactly the same time.

At one o'clock on Friday, October 25, Mr. and Mrs. Byers knelt in their son's Boston hospital room to join their prayers with Kathryn Kuhlman's in Pittsburgh. At the same time, Robert Byers' sister was praying for him in a church some sixty miles from Boston.

Then a strange thing happened.

"We all fell asleep," Kathryn Kuhlman said. "The young man fell asleep in his hospital bed. His parents fell asleep. Later they discovered that his sister fell asleep at the same time."

"Asleep?" I repeated quizzically.

"Well," the evangelist drawled, with an enigmatic smile, "we knew God was going to do a good work, and a sense of 'resting-faith' came upon all involved. Psalm 127:2 states: 'For so He giveth His beloved sleep.' "

Robert Byers did not need the lung surgery. He made a complete recovery.

12
The Importance of
Being Kathryn

Once I asked some of Kathryn Kuhlman's followers what was the greatest miracle in her ministry, and one of them replied: "Miss Kuhlman. She's the greatest miracle of all."

But why Kathryn Kuhlman?

This is the question most often put by people after they have been introduced to the Kuhlman healing ministry.

Is there something intrinsic in Kathryn Kuhlman, they ask, that sets her apart from other religious leaders? Or did providence give her this healing ministry by sheer divine arbitrariness? What makes her what she is?

Kathryn Kuhlman herself repeatedly says: "I have nothing to do with these healings. The miracles are produced by the power of God. And you can't analyze why God does things any more than you can analyze God himself. I am utterly dependent on the mercy and compassion of God."

Yet, despite her patently sincere disclaimers—and she has a real fear, as I've mentioned, that self-puffery in any form would cause her to lose The Power—Kathryn Kuhlman clearly *does* have something to do with the healings.

Such phenomena do not attend every clergyman who preaches the power of faith to heal. Why her?

An observer might guess that if any human quality could explain her astounding ministry it would be her love for people. Her followers frequently comment on her great compassion and care for people.

"Miss Kuhlman loves people back to health," was the way one woman put it. Another mentioned that the evangelist's deepest compassion seems to pour out on elderly people and children. She often weeps when praying for a sick child.

The evangelist told me once that nothing touches her quite so much as a little old lady who needs healing.

"When I see those hands so calloused from a lifetime of hard work, my heart just melts," she said. "And you know, whenever I feel that kind of compassion, invariably the person's healed."

The personality of Kathryn Kuhlman, what makes her what she is, defies full explanation. One can get glimmerings of truth about her, though. Before I ever met her, I discussed with a friend what I expected to find.

"If Kathryn Kuhlman is a genuine charismatic healer," I said, "I predict that certain things will be true of her.

"First, she'll be a particular kind of person. Since psychic powers probably are aboriginal and atavistic, she will be a woman who follows her instincts—in other words, is in close touch with her own unconscious. She will be naïve rather than sophisticated. She will be emotionally warm, outgoing, with a great openness toward other people. She will not be analytically minded—certainly not toward the power behind the healings.

"Second, since the freeing of the unconscious is a usual condition for the release of psychic power, there will be an indication of it in some form or degree. In other words, trance or at least a state of dissocation.

"Third, since any psychic gift rarely operates to the exclusion of similar gifts, there will be manifestations other than healing in her ministry—telepathy, clairvoyance, possibly precognition."

My predictions proved accurate. Kathryn Kuhlman fits into the general pattern, psychologically speaking, of psychically gifted people. Although she knows nothing about formal parapsychology, she has an instinctive understanding of the dynamics of the unconscious. As in many charismatic personalities, her conscious mind (read "theology") is often contradicted by her unconscious mind (read "the promptings of the Spirit"). The latter always wins. Her heart, if you like, rules her head.

On a rational level, as what I've reported thus far should make abundantly plain, she is as baffled, even confused, by the healings as anyone else is. But on the intuitive level, she knows more than she knows she knows.

There are parallels between the mystery at work in Kathryn Kuhlman's miracle services and that of Lourdes. In both cases, the people who come are often *in extremis*. They are suffering from mortal illnesses or from chronic ailments for which doctors have given up hope of cure. These people have reached the end of their physical and emotional resources. Their illnesses have become intolerable. They cannot any longer accept life in this condition, and yet they cannot accept death.

In this desperate state—too miserable to live and too frightened to die (which is perhaps about as good a definition of hell as one could ask for)—they find Kathryn Kuhlman. In her services, under the spell of her personality, a transference takes place. They surrender themselves to the unconditional love that is offered to them by the evangelist as God's representative. They are enabled to overcome their sense of alienation from life, from God, from their fellow human beings.

In the miracle services a community of love and acceptance is created. People feel secure enough to lay aside the barriers of fear, distrust, and egotism that have shut them off not only from fruitful contact with their fellow men but from their own deeper selves. There is a yielding up of self-isolation. The individual loses himself in the group, the symbol of the loving family where one is accepted in spite of his faults and sins. He identifies with the needs of others. He sometimes forgets his own illness, his own need, in praying for someone else whose need is greater. In this self-forgetfulness, as it happens, he is healed. If he already has found healing himself, he is praying that others may find the same great blessing.

Kathryn Kuhlman expresses her healing power in formulas that are natural to her, and to her congregations—the thought forms of a traditionalist theology. For her, the healing force is "the power of God," which works through "faith in Jesus Christ." In psychological terms, this could be translated: Love is the healing power and it is released by trust, commitment, and self-surrender.

There is a paradox about Kathryn Kuhlman's ministry which I've described on occasion as a sort of "uncertainty principle"; namely, that the more you think you can rationally analyze the healing power, the further away from it you get. One can understand it (approximately anyway) but not be able to use it; or one can use it (as Kathryn Kuhlman does) but not be able to understand it. Rational analysis in the area of faith is often like the electron microscope, which kills the organisms it makes visible.

Yet we are prompted to try to understand more clearly the why of Kathryn Kuhlman, even though we realize that we are up against an ultimate mystery. The ideal person to attempt such a clarification would be one who combined expertise in psychology with wisdom in understanding human beings (the two are not necessarily synonymous), and moreover one with an appreciation of the theological issues involved. Such a person is Don Gross.

Dr. Gross—whose proper name is "Don" and not, as well-intentioned people keep assuming, "Donald"—is an Episcopal priest with academic degrees in physics, theology, and psychology, including a Harvard doctorate in the psychology of religion. A profound student of the thought of Carl Jung, he wrote his Ph.D. thesis on a Jungian analysis of New Testament exorcism.

A long-time resident of Pittsburgh who served as rector of a suburban parish for several years, he is now Executive Director (and Founder) of the Pittsburgh Pastoral Institute, a clinic where disturbed people are counseled by psychologically oriented clergymen, and religiously oriented psychiatrists. I talked with Dr. Gross, a cerebral-looking man in his forties, with thinning hair and spectacles and a mouth that breaks easily into a relaxed grin, in September 1968. The main interview was in his office at the Pittsburgh Pastoral Institute adjacent to Emmanuel Episcopal Church in the heart of the city. We also talked at length in his suburban home.

Dr. Gross has been active in the revival of spiritual healing in the Episcopal Church, and is the author of a significant book on the subject, *The Case for Spiritual Healing*. Dr. E. B. Henry, the physician whose healing in a Kathryn Kuhlman service was described earlier, was his father-in-law. For almost the entire length of the evangelist's stay in Pittsburgh, Don Gross has been in a position to study her ministry.

In a long interview, for which he made time in his incredibly busy schedule, he talked with me about his impressions and assessment of the Kuhlman phenomenon. He spoke as a psychologist and a theologian, stressing that in his mind there is no conflict between the two. They are merely two sides of the same truth.

"My feeling," said Dr. Gross, leaning back in his chair and tapping his fingertips together, "is that the healings of Kathryn Kuhlman are connected with the collective unconscious of Jung, and that in the healing services there is a tremendous investment of psychological energy—and I'm speaking purely psychologically here—in what is represented by archetypal symbols having to do with God, Christ, and the Holy Spirit."

Archetypes, or archetypal symbols, in Jung's thought are universal images that have existed in the collective unconscious of mankind from remotest times. The profoundest and most important are those representing fundamental religious concepts or realities.

"This area of the archetypes," Dr. Gross continued, "is one which Jung referred to on certain occasions as *psychoid*, which is an interesting word because it means psychelike. It is like the mind, but is not directly accessible to consciousness, only through the intermediary of symbols.

"I have a hunch that this archetypal or psychoid area is the substratum of, and the connecting link between, consciousness on the one hand, and the physical world on the other. And the mind-body problem is even more difficult than supposed, because it's not really a dichotomy—mind and body—but a trichotomy in which there is an inaccessible intermediary between these two.

"Because we can't perceive the psychoid area, it's very hard to describe. Perhaps we can put it this way: The physical world we perceive as something outside the sensing organism, and the psychological world we perceive inwardly, but the archetypal or psychoid world, which is the substratum, we don't perceive in any manner and cannot in principle perceive. We come in contact with it only through the universal symbols from the collective unconscious called archetypes.

"These symbols have the capacity to attract to themselves, if the conditions in life are right, an enormous amount of psychological or, in this case, psychoid energy which can translate itself, I think, into actual physical effects. In fact, it may manifest as a completely creative act of new matter coming into being. I think my father-in-law's healing was a case in which there was re-creation of bone so that his clavicle knit after failing to calcify for eighteen months or so.

"And there are other cases in which the opposite seems to happen; the annihilation of matter, as, for example, when a tumor disappears. Here, energy that would normally be present in the physical world collapses out of it into the psychoid world.

"It is the same process working in opposite ways."

What role does Kathryn Kuhlman play in the release of this psychoid energy?

"She is the focus," Dr. Gross replied, "who draws together the energy of the assembled crowd. She is also the focus, I think, for people who are not even physically present in the service because, in the collective unconscious, time and space relationships change. Time is not sequential on that level of reality as it is here, and space relationships are different so that people who are aware of one another are somehow together in spite of separating distance.

"Kathryn Kuhlman is the catalyst who triggers the liberation of the psychoid energies latent in the congregation."

What makes her such a catalyst?

"Ah," murmured Dr. Gross with a smile, "that has to do

with her whole life history which I don't know in full detail. However, I would like to speculate on the psychodynamics of it. But I want to make one thing clear at this point: I do not consider that any psychological descriptions I offer undermine any spiritual interpretations. They are complementary, not contradictory.

"Kathryn Kuhlman is an extraordinarily creative woman to have accomplished what she has, particularly with the limitations of education and opportunity in her early life. What may have happened is that this intense person—and she has unusual intensity and energy—looking forward to marriage and family life, in which a woman has her normal creative activity in the bearing and raising of children, is frustrated. There is a great and painful collapse of her hopes and of her wish to love and be loved. At this point she turns to God as her love object. She is going to spiritualize the energy that would have gone into marriage and family life and devote herself instead to another kind of love, love of the Heavenly Father.

"I would guess that she loved her earthly father devotedly and hoped in marriage to find the fulfillment of that first great love in her life. Out of her deep frustration of this hope she turns to the Heavenly Father who won't disappoint her.

"She is very hurt, and in looking for healing for her own heart finds that one way of being healed is to become a channel of healing to others. Sometimes the best way to make up for a disappointment in love is to give love. So, as Kathryn Kuhlman becomes a channel for spreading God's love to others, she receives that love herself and her heart is healed.

"Instead of receiving love from one person in marriage, she turns out to be the center of the adoration of many people.

"Mind you, this love from many is not fully satisfying. Like all public figures, Kathryn Kuhlman says 'I live a lonely life; I'm either with the crowd or I'm all alone.' But the difference is that Kathryn Kuhlman is not really completely alone, but alone with God. She has found such an experience of God's love and presence that it fills the void which tempts some public figures even to suicide. And it is this experience of God's love that makes her charismatic—the sense of God's love and presence radiates from her."

What about the evangelist's feeling of being out-of-the-body during the miracle services, what she calls being "caught up in the Spirit"?

"This," declared Dr. Gross with a knowing chuckle, "is beautifully reminiscent of the ecstatic state reported by some medieval saints and mystics. The root of the word ecstasy from the Greek means 'standing out of oneself.' And it is by this standing out of herself that Kathryn Kuhlman becomes the clear channel through which the healing power flows.

"However, the channel is not merely one-way. It is not merely that the power of God flows somehow through Kathryn Kuhlman and out to the people but also that the people's devotion somehow is channeled through her to God. And I think this is the key to the healings. For even though one individual in the service might not have to have much devotion to get healed, the whole group has to have the devotion to create an atmosphere in which the healings can happen.

"Psychologically, it is interesting how the psychoid power that heals is built up in the services. First, Kathryn Kuhlman gives the example of her devotion. She gets people to stand up and tell about their healings, which is intended to inspire expectation in the others. A feeling of numinous, awesome wonder is created as the stories of God's healing power are recounted. And this is, for me, the theological essence of a miracle—it is a sign and a wonder proclaiming that God is alive and loving and able to help those who seek Him.

"The atmosphere of faith and expectation is further built up by the singing of hymns which stress the greatness of God, and the power of simple faith. These hymns are repeated over and over with actual hypnotic effect until the deep unconscious is touched and the people's energies are tremendously mobilized.

"The hymns repeat the archetypal themes of God, Christ, and the Holy Spirit who heals. It is love that heals, but love channeled through the archetypal symbols. The effectiveness of a living symbol is its capacity to channel psychological or psychoid energy. The greater the emotional intensity which the symbol arouses, the greater the devotion and energy it channels. Such spiritual symbols as God, Christ, and the Holy Spirit attract tremendous devotion and thus are capable of channeling tremendous healing energy."

In this drama of awesome symbols—perhaps the deepest and most powerful in man's ancestral consciousness—what does Kathryn Kuhlman symbolize?

"I've been thinking about that," admitted Dr. Gross, tapping his fingertips together. "She does take on archetypal symbolism. It's interesting that she is a feminine image because femininity in the language of symbols has to do with maternity. In a sense, she is the spiritual mother of the whole crowd. The maternal image here is combined with the paternal image of God. We have the two polarities—paternity and maternity. This is the divine marriage, so to speak, as when we call the Church the Bride of Christ, or refer to Mother Church.

"Out of the marriage between the image of the Heavenly

Father and the spiritual mother comes new birth. The healings are new births, if you like. They are the fruit of the spiritual union between God and the maternal image.

"I'm reminded here of Lourdes, where the Virgin is the mother of all who come seeking healing."

Dr. Gross remarked that he wanted to return to the evangelist's out-of-the-body experiences when the miracles are happening.

"Her sense of dissociation is exactly what I would have expected. She is not completely out of it, you notice, as she would be if she were in a hypnotic trance where you remember nothing. Instead she is halfway between consciousness and unconsciousness, precisely in that in-between area where you get the interplay of the two. It is a hypnoidal state that she is in, neither complete consciousness nor complete unconsciousness. The bringing together of the two touches the whole being and maximizes the potential for healing.

"In this hypnoidal state, I would expect her to have telepathy or clairvoyance by which she is able to diagnose illnesses. I wouldn't expect her to be 100 percent accurate, however."

Dr. Gross suggested that Kathryn Kuhlman's supernormal awareness of when and to whom a healing is occurring might be interpreted in terms of Jung's concept of synchronicity—two events which are linked meaningfully but noncausally.

"The collective unconscious not only lacks the normal time and space relationships but cause and effect relationships too," he said. "It links together separate points in time and space.

"The collective unconscious, as the area of the psychoid, links events in the psychological world with events in the physical world. The events are paired, are synchronous.

Either they are absolutely simultaneous or almost simultaneous, or, like a prediction and its fulfillment, they match. In this sense, they are synchronous or equivalent. Yet the two events are not directly perceived to be causally related in the sense that one is the result of the other. They are what I would call meaningful—and that word is very important—coincidences.

"So when Kathryn Kuhlman said of my father-in-law, Dr. Henry, 'There's a man receiving a healing, I see a lump the size of a walnut beginning to dissolve, etc.,' this coincided with the healing. Her announcement coincided with the event. The meaning of the event is seen through the actual coincidence, and we are impressed and ask how did she know, and this gives us the awesome sense of the holiness and love of God. This feeling always accompanies this archetypal kind of event.

"When in her semidissociated state the evangelist finds things popping into her awareness which in many cases correspond to actual events, this is the phenomenon of synchronicity."

Why are skeptics sometimes healed in Kathryn Kuhlman's services while believers are not?

Dr. Gross furrowed his brow and adjusted his glasses.

"The thing lacking in these cases of so-called skeptics is overt faith," he said slowly, "but what goes on in people unconsciously doesn't always correspond with what goes on consciously. I've discovered, for example, that most, if not all, atheists really don't disbelieve in God.

"I once counseled a boy who was an avowed atheist. But he was really angry with God because he had lost his brother from leukemia when his brother was a child, and he had never gotten over it. He was still angry, still full of reaction formation, as the analysts say. Like many skeptics, he protested too much. The tipoff was that his favorite company for discussing things was clergymen. He was always going to church.

"Atheists are devoutly religious people who are fighting it. They are reacting against or are angry with God's representatives, or something that represents God to them, or some immature idea of God."

A person who is closed against healing on the conscious level, then, may be wide open to it at the deeper levels of his personality. And since, as Jung once remarked, fanaticism chiefly compensates for secret doubts, the militant atheist may be the closest thing to a true believer. Conversely, some who advertise themselves as true believers may actually be the furthest from the kingdom of God. Man looks at the outward appearance, but the Great Psychoanalyst looks in the heart.

Dr. Gross disavowed the dogma of some revivalists that since faith equals healing, the absence of healing must equal the absence of faith.

"This is a very great oversimplification," he said emphatically, "which leaves many people feeling very guilty if they're not healed. The fact that they're not healed may have nothing to do with them personally. It may, or it may not. We don't know. Such a false teaching is responsible for much of the justified criticism of the healing ministries of some.

"Such a simplistic view isn't sound theologically. Paul the Apostle wasn't healed of his thorn in the flesh, as he called it, and he actually related this not to lack of faith but to his need to be humble. He had to be reminded that he was frail and human for his own good.

"If Kathryn Kuhlman were ever to get self-important, it would kill her ministry and I'm sure she knows this. Her recurring dream of going to a service and finding only empty seats expresses her anxiety that she may lose the gift and become spiritually barren, unfruitful. Her un-conscious is giving her a warning to guard against this temptation. The dream is a message to herself from her-self, and she's getting the message."

No person, however devoted or saintly, is either impec-cable or infallible, Dr. Gross observed.

"I think Kathryn Kuhlman has made mistakes. Perhaps she has felt at times that someone was healed when in fact it wasn't so. Perhaps at times she has been too quick to jump to conclusions and to be guided by the intuition when the intuition in that instance wasn't right.

"I have seen examples, too, of some of her followers who were very uncharitable toward other people and undid the whole purpose of her ministry, which is to reconcile men to God and to each other."

What about the warnings by critics of faith healing that a ministry such as Kathryn Kuhlman's can harm people as well as help them?

"Yes, it's said that if neurotics are forced to yield up their physical symptoms under the stimulus of a faith healer, they are liable to develop suicidal tendencies or re-place the former symptoms with new and more devastating ones," Dr. Gross remarked.

"Well, this depends on what the symptom means to the person. I admit that this sort of thing is conceivable. But the issue here has to do with whether it is primarily the symptom that is affected or whether there is some kind of transaction that affects the whole personality. I can imagine people in certain emotional states who might lose a cer-tain symptom, but then the underlying conflicts would cause the problem to be displaced to some other area of their life. However, in such cases, the people didn't have a total reorientation of personality as many do in Kathryn Kuhlman's services."

It is this radical reorientation of personal values that supremely marks Kathryn Kuhlman's healing ministry as an "authentic" one, says Dr. Gross.

"There are two ways of establishing the authenticity of her ministry. The first is to investigate the healings and establish whether something genuine has happened. By this norm the headings are authentic.

"But there is a higher form of authenticity. I'm sure Kathryn Kuhlman is more concerned about spiritual authenticity. She wants to see that this is not just some kind of odd physical healing, but that it glorifies God and people's lives are changed by it so that they become more loving and more aware of the presence of God.

"If it makes them witnesses to the power of Christ and inspires them to carry on his work, then it is authentic."

The healing of his father-in-law brought this dimension of spiritual change, says Dr. Gross.

"Although he was a devout person in his heart and an elder in the Presbyterian Church, Dr. Henry, as far as his medical experience was concerned, had never seen anything like a miraculous healing. He was unprepared to accept it. But of course when it happened to him, he had to believe it. It was a complete surprise to him. All of a sudden there was this personal, awesome quality to God's healing power. It wasn't any longer merely a mechanical, impersonal biological force. There was a sense of God's personal providence which it brought home to him and which was a definite step forward in his spiritual development.

"It is significant that Dr. Henry was healed through self-forgetfulness which was characteristic of his whole life as a doctor. He was always deeply concerned about other people. And it was while he was praying for somebody else, his wife, in Kathryn Kuhlman's meeting, that he was healed himself.

"So often it happens this way. By losing ourselves we find ourselves."

❖❖❖❖

Kathryn Kuhlman's ministry is institutionalized in the Kathryn Kuhlman Foundation, a religious, charitable, non-profit corporation. She receives a salary stipulated by the board of the Foundation.

In addition to financing the evangelist's ministry (besides her public meetings she is heard on some one hundred radio stations and appears on nearly fifty television stations), the Foundation subsidizes a spectrum of humanitarian activities.

Needy families receive groceries and other provisions from a well-stocked commissary. More than one person has told me of how quickly practical assistance came when they asked the Kathryn Kuhlman Foundation for help. One Pittsburgh poultry dealer received a check for $1,900 from the Foundation for chickens provided to needy families in a single month.

By a system of scholarships and student loans, the Kathryn Kuhlman Foundation has financed the education of young people enrolled in a variety of courses of study at Wheaton College (Illinois), Pennsylvania State University, the University of Pittsburgh, the Cincinnati Conservatory of Music, the Carnegie Institute of Technology, and other institutions.

The Foundation has donated more than $40,000 to the Western Pennsylvania School for the Blind. It also has supported a farm in rural Pennsylvania for the rehabilitation of teen-aged drug addicts from America's concrete jungles.

At present, twenty-one missionary churches and church-related institutions (children's homes, schools) are subsidized by the Kathryn Kuhlman Foundation—one for each year of the evangelist's ministry in Pittsburgh. These are located in such places as Corn Island, Nicaragua; San Isidro, Costa Rica; Thakurpukur, India; Macao, China; Cotonu, Dahomey, West Africa; Taipei, Formosa; Kuala Lumpur, Malaysia; Surabaja, Indonesia; and Saigon, South Vietnam.

In 1967 Kathryn Kuhlman received the keys of the city from Pittsburgh's civic fathers, to commemorate the twentieth anniversary of her ministry there.

The evidence presented in this book establishes, it seems to me, a strong case for the authenticity of Kathryn Kuhlman's healing ministry. Let me sum up.

In the first place, her ministry has won the respect, largely, of civic and religious leaders in the place where she has worked for more than two decades. In her early days she knew the criticism that is the lot of most evangelists (and she does not completely escape it even today), but this, on the whole, has given way to positive recognition.

The fact that the evangelist holds her weekly Pittsburgh miracle services in the prominent First Presbyterian Church there, by invitation of the minister and elders, speaks for itself.

In 1964, when I asked the then Episcopal bishop of Pittsburgh, Rt. Rev. Austin Pardue, about Kathryn Kuhlman, he said: "Her ministry certainly has made a huge impression on this city."

Famed missionary leader, teacher, and literacy expert Dr. Frank Laubach has called Kathryn Kuhlman "the greatest channel for love and healing I know of in the world today."

Judge Samuel A. Weiss of the Allegheny County Court

of Common Pleas publicly praised the evangelist's ministry as "a unique one which has had its influence upon
thousands."

Kathryn Kuhlman's healings have proved to be more
substantial than those of the typical itinerant revivalist,
which more often than not last only as long as the spell of
the healer's personality. Some of her healings have lasted
for more than twenty years. Often they are accompanied by
a dramatic and permanent change for the better in the
individual's character and way of life as well.

Moreover, there exists a solid, impressive core of medically attested evidence that a substantial number of the
healings, allowing for every conceivable normal hypothesis, appear to be genuinely beyond scientific explanation.

Lung cancer (Paul Gunn) does not retreat before mere
emotionalism. A club foot (Karen George) does not yield
to the power of suggestion—even if an infant were susceptible to suggestion. Mitral stenosis (Mila Litten) may
be correctable by open heart surgery but not by spontaneous remission. Blindness due to a deep corneal burn
(George Orr) can hardly be put down as a case of wrong
diagnosis. A cracked collarbone which refused to calcify
for eighteen months (Dr. E. B. Henry) is not a hysterical
ailment. A corneal lesion attested to by two ophthalmolo-
gists (the four-year-old boy treated by Dr. Clair King) is
not imaginary.

There is corroboration from other sources that Kathryn
Kuhlman's healings are possible. When one is confronted
by similar reports from independent researchers, the clear
implication is that an objective phenomenon lies behind
the reports. Parapsychologists have established a *prima
facie* case for psychokinesis—mind over matter, the mind's
supernormal ability to act on physical objects at a distance.

Experiments at Duke University over a period of several

years indicated scientifically that some people can influence the fall of dice by will power. The essence of at least one kind of prayer is desire ("Prayer," says an old hymn, "is the heart's sincere desire, unuttered or expressed"), and there is no essential difference in this sense, between causing dice to fall in a certain way by mental concentration and regressing a tumor by prayer.

There is evidence that prayer as such does release a force which stimulates healing, to be found from experiments at McGill University—where plants grew more rapidly and robustly, and laboratory animals exhibited faster healing of wounds, after prayer.

Other curious phenomena, which are eminently familiar to parapsychologists, occur in Kathryn Kuhlman's meetings. Her ability to diagnose symptoms intuitively strongly suggests clairvoyance, a form of extrasensory perception documented by numerous careful parapsychologists and psychical researchers. That a person who exhibits healing power should also manifest other forms of psychic phenomena is to be expected.

It seems to me that, after weighing the data, the most plausible conclusion is that healings, for which there is no adequate normal explanation, do occur in Kathryn Kuhlman's ministry. They are "miracles."

My personal view of Kathryn Kuhlman has grown out of my acquaintance with her for more than five years. My wife and I have talked with her for long hours, watched her in public, and relaxed with her over dinner.

We have seen the devotion of her followers and noted that those who know her best are the most devoted. We have discovered that she has a puckish sense of humor. She is very much a woman, in her fondness for fine clothes, for instance. She takes a healthy delight and a childlike pride in "the nice things" her material success has made possible. She sees no virtue in returning to the extreme poverty of her early days, nor do I.

But I believe her unreservedly when she says that she would rather give up every material thing than lose her sense of the presence of God.

Nobody can light up a room or an immense auditorium as Kathryn Kuhlman does. She is wired for a million volts.

Nobody else conveys such an easy impression of being on intimate terms with God.

In my career as a newspaperman I've rubbed elbows with the great and near-great, but when I am asked who, of all those I've met, has impressed me most, there is only one possible answer: Kathryn Kuhlman.

In my judgment she is a saint.

In some singular, mysterious way she has transmuted personal sorrow into a universal love for her fellow human beings.

She is one of the most extraordinary Christian mystics and clairvoyants of our time. Yet if you told her this, she would ask you what in the world you meant, and probably flatly deny it.

She is the greatest charismatic healer of our time. And one of the greatest ever known.

She is the most remarkable person I know.

Bibliography

BENDIT, PHOEBE D. and LAURENCE J. *Man Incarnate: A Study of the Vital Etheric Field.* London: The Theosophical Publishing House. 1957.

BRADEN, CHARLES S. *These Also Believe.* New York: The Macmillan Company. 1949.

BYCHOWSKI, GUSTAV and LOUISE J. DESPERT, editors. *Specialized Techniques in Psychotherapy* (especially the chapter "Psychotherapeutic Techniques in Psychosomatic Medicine"). New York: Basic Books. 1952.

CARREL, ALEXIS D. *Man, the Unknown.* New York: Harper & Brothers. 1935.

CLINE, BARBARA LOVETT. *The Questioners.* New York: Thomas Y. Crowell Company. 1965.

CRANSTON, RUTH. *The Miracle of Lourdes.* New York: McGraw-Hill. 1955.

DE LAZLO, VIOLET S., editor. *The Basic Writings of C. G. Jung.* New York: The Modern Library. 1959.

DE LA WARR, GEORGE and DOUGLAS BAKER. *Biomagnetism.* Oxford: Delawarr Laboratories Ltd. 1967.

DESMOND, SHAW. *The Power of Faith Healing.* New York: Liveright Publishing Corporation. 1957.

DONIGER, SIMON, editor. *Religion and Health.* New York: Association Press. 1958.

DUNBAR, FLANDERS. *Mind and Body: Psychosomatic Medicine.* New York: Random House. 1947.

EDDINGTON, ARTHUR. *The Nature of the Physical World.* New York: The Macmillan Company. 1928.

EISENBUD, JULE. *The World of Ted Serios.* New York: William Morrow & Company, Inc. 1967.

175

ESTABROOKS, G. H. *Hypnotism*. New York: E. P. Dutton & Co. 1943.

FODOR, NANDOR. *The Search for the Beloved*. New York: Hermitage Press, Inc. 1949.

GARRETT, EILEEN J., editor. *Beyond the Five Senses*. (especially the chapters "Faith Healing at Lourdes" and "Diagnosis: Miracle"). Philadelphia, New York: J. B. Lippincott Company. 1957.

GROSS, DON H. *The Case for Spiritual Healing*. New York: Thomas Nelson & Sons. 1958.

JUNG, CARL G. *Memories, Dreams, Reflections*. New York: Pantheon Books. 1961.

KUHLMAN, KATHRYN. *God Can Do It Again*. Englewood Cliffs, N.J.: Prentice-Hall, Inc. 1969.

————. *I Believe in Miracles*. Englewood Cliffs, N.J.: Prentice-Hall, Inc. 1962.

KUHN, LESLEY and SALVATORE RUSSO, editors. *Modern Hypnosis*. Hollywood: Wilshire Book Co. 1958.

LE CRON, LESLIE M. *Self-Hypnotism*. Englewood Cliffs, N.J.: Prentice-Hall, Inc. 1964.

LEURET, FRANÇOIS and HENRI BON. *Modern Miraculous Cures*. New York: Farrar, Straus & Cudahy, Inc. 1957.

LOEHR, FRANKLIN. *The Power of Prayer on Plants*. New York: The New American Library. 1969.

MARCUSE, F. L. *Hypnosis: Fact and Fiction*. Baltimore: Penguin Books. 1959.

MURRAY, GEOFFREY. *Frontiers of Healing*. London: Max Parrish. 1958.

NEAL, EMILY GARDINER. *A Reporter Finds God Through Spiritual Healing*. New York: Morehouse-Barlow Co. 1956.

RHINE, J. B. *New Frontiers of the Mind*. New York: Farrar & Rhinehart. 1937.

RHINE, LOUISA E. *ESP in Life and Lab*. New York: The Macmillan Company. 1967.

ROBERTS, ORAL. *If You Need Healing Do These Things*. Tulsa, Oklahoma: Healing Waters, Inc. 1954.

SARGENT, WILLIAM. *Battle for the Mind*. London: Wm. Heinemann Ltd. 1957.

SKOTTOWE, IAN. *Clinical Psychiatry*. London: J. & A. Churchill Ltd. 1964.

SLAUGHTER, FRANK. *Medicine for Moderns.* New York: Julian Messner, Inc. 1947.

Some Unrecognized Factors in Medicine. London: Theosophical Research Center. 1939.

SPRAGGETT, ALLEN. *The Unexplained.* New York: The New American Library. 1967.

STAFFORD, ANN. *Bernadette and Lourdes.* London: Hodder and Stoughton. 1967.

STERN, KARL. *The Third Revolution.* New York: Harcourt, Brace and Company. 1954.

TOURNIER, PAUL. *The Healing of Persons.* New York: Harper & Row. 1965.

WAVELL, STEWART, AUDREY BUTT, and NINA EPTON. *Trances.* London: George Allen & Unwin Ltd. 1966.

WEATHERHEAD, LESLIE D. *Psychology in the Service of the Soul.* London: The Epworth Press. 1929.

———. *Psychology, Religion and Healing.* New York, Nashville: Abingdon Press. 1951.

———. *Wounded Spirits.* London: Hodder and Stoughton Ltd. 1962.

WEST, DONALD J. *Eleven Lourdes Miracles.* New York: Helix Press. 1959.

WITTKOFSKI, JOSEPH. *The Pastoral Use of Hypnotic Technique.* New York: The Macmillan Company. 1961.

WOLBERG, LOUIS. *Medical Hypnosis* (two volumes). New York: Grune & Stratton. 1948.

WOLFE, BERNARD and RAYMOND ROSENTHAL. *Hypnotism Comes of Age.* Indianapolis, New York: The Bobbs-Merrill Co. 1948.

WOODARD, CHRISTOPHER. *A Doctor Heals by Faith.* London: Max Parrish & Co. Ltd. 1959.

WORRALL, AMBROSE and OLGA N. *The Gift of Healing.* New York: Harper & Row. 1965.

About the Author

ALLEN SPRAGGETT, who has been called Canada's leading ESP expert, arranged and moderated the now famous television séance in which former Bishop James Pike said he contacted his dead son through medium Arthur Ford. Educated at Queen's University at Kingston, Ontario, Mr. Spraggett was a parish minister for eight years. In 1962 he became religion editor of *The Toronto Daily Star,* Canada's largest newspaper, and has been a columnist with *The Star* since 1968. A member of the Society for Psychical Research in London, he has appeared on a number of radio and television shows as an expert in ESP. Mr. Spraggett knows many of the leading parapsychologists of our time, and has had readings with famous psychics in Canada, the United States, England, France, and Italy. He is married and the father of two sons and three daughters. His first book, *The Unexplained,* was published in 1967.